From Sympathy

(pseudo)

To Empathy

*A story of a 23 year-old Asian American who helped in
a local orphanage in rural Uganda for 2 weeks*

By Ambrose Tse

Ambrose Tse

ISBN: 979-8-9909973-1-8

For privacy reasons, some names, locations, and dates may have been changed.

Book Cover & Illustrations by Studio 83

First Edition 2024

"You do not delight in sacrifice, or I would bring it; you do not take pleasure in burnt offerings. The sacrifices of God are a broken spirit; a broken and contrite heart, O God, you will not despise."

Psalms 51: 16-17

3

Ambrose Tse

4

Table of Contents

Ambrose Tse

Preface

There is no easy way to write about preventable pain and suffering among children. This book is not intended to be written just as a religious genre. It can be read by someone as a travelogue, or for those who wants to seriously think about life and death when something tragic happens. The writer chose to narrate his story in an unconventional way not primarily for the purpose of entertaining his audiences, showing bitterness or sarcasm towards human or supernatural beings, or pointing out how big the needs are in developing countries. Rather, at the end it was about the attitude he adopted to deal with life going forward in the midst of both triumphs and failures. The transformation was life-changing, and had compelled the author to share his idea via this method and channel.

It doesn't take a rich or famous icon to engage in the charitable causes reported in the news to make a difference in other people's lives. If someone as clumsy, ignorant, gullible, and politically insensitive as the author was able to survive and remember the lessons learned from participating in a mission trip that appeared to have gone astray in every aspect, how much more do you think can be accomplished if more people with a slightly heavier heart were willing to move beyond their comfort zone?

The ultimate, and always the most fundamental questions, to ask remain to be: "Who am I?", and "What matters the most in the world we are living in, aside from the security that we all so dearly held onto and chased after throughout our lives?"

I just can't seem to be able to ever move away from reiterating these old school talks.

Ambrose Tse

Prologue

To "live life to its fullest", Ambrose was no stranger in traveling overseas for fun, enjoying fine gourmet, and gaining access to the most up-to-date gadgets and fashion that gave him thrills and satisfaction in his early 20's. When an opportunity to help in an orphanage and a medical clinic in exciting Africa for two weeks knocked on the door while he was climbing the corporate ladder in the banking world, he quickly signed up to activate his "altruism" gene that would make his life even more colorful and complete. But problems started to arise and multiply once he left his own little world and landed in the middle of a jungle, where all of his preparations in advance were brutally thrown out of the window. What aggravated the situation even more was the irreconcilable differences between him and his teammates, who were mostly strangers to each other that came from all sorts of backgrounds, and each individual carried a personal agenda and a set of ideals of his or her own. When Ambrose was finally able to position himself and adjust to the wild and unexpected twists and turns created by the temporary external environment, it was almost time to pack up and go home. So what happened at the end? Was Ambrose able to accomplish the goals he had from the beginning? What lessons did he take away, if any? What long-term impact did this trip have on Ambrose's epiphany on making a difference in other people's lives as well as his own?

Unlike other stories that promote philanthropic virtues, "From Sympathy (*pseudo*) To Empathy" was a raw non-fictional account of the spiritual journey of an ordinary guy told in the first person point of view that was purposely written in colloquial language to reflect an accurate picture of the pressing conditions in a developing country. If Ambrose, someone who shares a ton of similarities with an average Joe, could reject complacency, strived to breathe some fresh air in the middle of the day, took a stab to face his own weaknesses, then eventually discover and make use of the small amount of his deeply embedded strength, courage, and creativity to genuinely "live life to its fullest" while encouraging others to consider doing the same, then so could anyone!

From Sympathy (pseudo) To Empathy

Chapter 01: Where's My "Al Bundy" Story?*

"Oh come on, this can't be right?!"

It was 5 minutes passed 6pm in the evening. I was sitting at my cubicle starring brainlessly at the colorful spreadsheet on the computer screen.

"Just 10 more minutes", I took a deep breath and told myself, "then I will be out of here".

There were only a handful of people left in the office, either working hard and struggling like me or making personal phone calls. Most of my colleagues had already left an hour ago.

I was tempted to get up, stretch, yawn, and pop my neck at the same time from my warm chair, but immediately gave up on that idea since I had no confidence that the yawning could cover all the weird noises I was deliberately making.

The quiet surrounding didn't help focus on wrapping up for the day. Instead, I opened up the web browser and clicked on the same link again for the third time within the last 10 hours.

No, it wasn't any dirty site. I would never take that kind of risk at work.

It was a page about a medical / children ministry trip to rural Uganda for the coming spring. It sounded like a really thrilling adventure for a good cause.

But my senses caught up right away: what could a bank auditor do at a medical clinic in the middle of a jungle?

The description of the trip read something like this: "*Be a part of a ground-breaking opportunity in this 'face-to-face' trip with the children of Uganda. Serve at a home orphanage, playing with and administering medical aid to its children. Also take part in prayer walking over this impoverished region, and encourage local believers in their ongoing Gospel work. This team is in partnership with FCA."*

So, let's see now: the part about playing with the children, prayer walking, and encouraging the locals sounded manageable.

Wait- here's the rest: *"Exact date: 4/28/03 to 5/13/03; Length: 1 to 2 weeks; Finances: $3,500 USD total, which included airfare, ground transportation, housing, meals, tips, in-country materials, airport taxes and insurance costs from SFO. Special early bird discount: $200 if all funds are in by 1/15/03".*

Okay, let me think through this again: I would need to come up with more than three grand in 2 months, go to no man's land with a group of strangers, and do something that I had never tried before?

Damn right. That was exactly what I wanted, if not crazier.

Since graduated from college in year 2000, my so call "career path" had been incredibly lousy: first I got a job as a "Personal Banker" (or "PB"), and then transferred internally to a "Collateral Asset-Based Examiner" (or "auditor") position after about a year. These titles sounded fancy, but what a "PB" does was to aggressively sell a bunch of junk to almost anyone who walked into a branch just to make a deposit, or to answer questions from some stuck-up mediocre average folks liked "how come your fees are so high compared to all other banks?". Being an auditor was relatively better, but the traveling and the office politics could drain so much of your energy that you would end up spending more time being frustrated than doing the actual auditing work itself.

So, I questioned about my life but couldn't really see where I was heading. I meant, I could hardly imagine running into someone that would tell me how he or she dreamed about becoming an auditor ever since he or she was a little kid. That just won't happen. I didn't know what was going to happen in the long run, but I definitely needed a break sooner or later.

Okay, enough self-justification. How about asking for some advices from the people around?

I told my family about this opportunity. My dad and sister didn't say much, and my mom smiled and didn't say anything either.

Talk about family support.

As much as I wanted to prove to them that I was serious and capable of doing something so out of the ordinary and meaningful, I felt that I needed a better reason to go other than making myself sounded like a hero. There are lots of "reasons" why someone goes on a mission trip: the sick and poor desperately needed help spiritually and financially; because this is mandated so in the Bible, and millions of other personal ideals. But for me, none of these seemed to suffice.

I had finally found the one and only reason to go, about a month later. It was like a natural call- it came quickly and without warning.

There was an annual 4-day retreat / conference in the Santa Cruz Mountains (about a 2-hour drive from San Francisco) right after Christmas that I had occasionally gone to for the past several years. It was an event designed for spiritual reorganization and primarily targeted to college students from overseas studying in the west coast. But I went anyway for a quiet place to think through this deal, especially when the early bird discount deadline for the trip was fast approaching.

During a workshop session on the second evening of the conference, the speaker shared about his personal experience in struggling to become a pastor in his mid-40's after working as an engineer for almost 20 years. Usually, one of the main themes for a conference of this nature was to urge people to go serve in East Asia. It totally made sense, after all.

My mind took off after the first few minutes of introduction and returned to my dilemma. The cluelessness still clouded over my head and it started to piss me off. I closed my eyes and prayed silently, in hopes that a voice from above would just give a short and sweet answer like: "Just go." or "What, are you nuts?"

No magic, of course. I reopened my eyes and gave the speaker the proper respect.

After about 45 seconds, the speaker suddenly said: "Well, you can certainly think about going to a short-term mission trip somewhere, like to *Africa*."

BAM!

Hey, wait a minute: what did he just say?! Wasn't he talking about his career transition? Why did he spill something so out of context?

I sat up straight on the chair, stunned. Soon, I realized what has happened and became very relieved and peaceful. The feeling was like finally being able to unload after a week-long constipation. Call me superstitious, but I had never ever had a prayer answered so directly and swiftly.

No more hesitation. It was time for some action.

****

The process was actually pretty smooth after making the decision to go: I called the organization and they told me that if I were sincerely interested, make a deposit first by 1/15/03, and pay the remaining balance a little later. So I immediately drafted a prayer

16

letter and distributed about 50 copies to the people I knew from church and my relatives to raise funds. The result was somewhat disappointing though: only half of the amount was raised. I couldn't complain much, given it was a short notice and I asked for more than three grand. At the end, I took care of the other half from my own piggy bank. By that time financing should NOT be an issue anymore.

Meanwhile, I asked my boss for 2 weeks of paid time off from 4/23/03 to 5/7/03. Presumably, there could be some problems because it was too early in the year to request for vacation, and my seniority was on the bottom of the list. But to my utter surprise, he was okay with it. Springtime was usually not a busy season, and our audits were all project-based. Another hurdle crossed.

Now, I started to become anxious about the strangers that I will be going to Uganda with. What if the organization was in fact a cult, or a bunch of crazy bum living in a hut also signed up to go? Damn, I should have thought about this earlier- so I busted out all the skills derived from my job: looked for audit trial online, checked for any inconsistencies in the materials they sent me, carefully scrutinize their mission statement, and asked around for the typical protocols of preparing and arranging a mission team by a credible organization.

No negative findings yet. Thank God. The best way to confirm my comfort level was to meet "face-to-face" with those that were going. That opportunity was coming up real soon at the first gathering in the organizer's home down in Modesto (don't mispronounce), near central California. It felt strange to be both excited and cautious.

****

The golden rule in avoiding any disappointment was not to have any expectations. I maintained my basic courtesy and refraining from laughing until I got back into the car at the end of the day. No offense against anyone in particular, but the team composition was somewhat "goofy", and this was perhaps the most appropriate adjective I could find. All I could say was that sometimes God seriously works in unpredictable and humorous ways.

Before I elaborate further, let's go back to the moment I rang the doorbell.

Thanks to free online directions from a popular website, I got lost and arrived late. A group of people were already seated in the living room getting ready to start. The environment was really casual, and everyone appeared to be quite friendly. Their "Brady Bunch" style hairdo and vintage clothing also promoted that impression.

It was only the first meeting. I didn't forget.

A humongous guy started playing with his guitar while some song sheets were being passed around. His name was Mick, a pastor going to Uganda with the team. Thanks to the music, songs, and lyrics, they have proved that my teammates were not some religious fanatics.

After some singing, Arlene, a lady in her 60's, who was the owner of the house and the chief organizer, stepped in to briefly introduce each of us to everyone else. Then, we went straight into discussing some of the logistics from basic overseas traveling information to personal preparations, as well as individual responsibilities within the group.

Little did I know, there were a few people joined from out-of-state and we would not see them until the departure date at the airport. They were: John, a retired banker from Oregon; Brenda, a special education teacher from the D.C. area; and Raeanne, a registered nurse from the Pacific Northwest. The other key missing person was the leader of the team named Don, who was in Dominican Republic at the time for another project. He was working for an organization called "FTFI" in cactus land, and "FCA" here in Modesto was the entity that partnered with this short-term mission trip "specialist".

The other new friends whom I will be going to Uganda with were: Pastor Mick from NorCal; Bob, an engineer in his early 30's from the Bay Area; Doctor Doug, a local pediatrician in Modesto; Arlene, the founder of FCA, and June, Shirley, Allison, and Denise. I never got their personal info, but believed some of them were either homemakers or work for FCA. A few of them knew each other already, while most, like me, didn't know anyone at all. It turned out that most of them had never been on a mission trip before, and some had not even been out of the country.

My anxiety came back to haunt me. So I raised my hand and asked a question.

I forgot what I precisely asked about and what the answer was. But I did remember the expressions on most people's faces when I started talking. They all appeared surprised and tried to give the best of their attention to make everyone felt welcome. Funny how I have only occasionally experienced this kind of awkwardness in the air outside of the Bay Area. There wasn't much you can do about it, so I eventually learned to accept it.

The reality was that I was being seen differently. But guess what? It didn't matter, because this kind of stereotype turned out to work for my advantage when I was in Uganda.

As the discussion continued, it was obvious that nothing much had been planned or decided in terms of the working agenda while in Uganda. A bunch of them were worrying about the post-911 safety issues for traveling overseas, or what mandatory medical shots to take within the next couple of months. After about 3 hours, the only productive consensus reached was to have another meeting in late March to spend more time for discussion. Meanwhile, we could email each other for any questions or concerns.

Crap.

Let's just say that I was being too critical and ideal sometimes. The good part was that there were still 8 weeks left to prepare for the trip itself and to work out any differences between me and the teammates. They may "think things differently", but I was optimistic to see that if I could keep an open mind, I should be able to learn a lot from the perspectives of these older folks.

Yes, that was indeed my thought; I wasn't being conceited or sarcastic.

The outcome from the first meeting prompted me to spend more time researching about Uganda, the biblical basis for short-term missions, and relationships skills enhancements. I must confess that after being an auditor for awhile, I have slowly lost the kind of patience to deal with people from all walks of life when I was still a personal banker.

I bought a 200-page guide from Borders bookstore that talked about the history, background, and all the current factual information about Uganda. The country was once described as the "Pearl of Africa" because of its rich natural resources stemmed from and nurtured by the Nile River, where it geographically began in a Ugandan town named Jinja close to Lake Victoria. Lake Victoria is the largest lake of the continent, bordered by Kenya, Tanzania, and Uganda. In the late 1800's, Uganda became a British colony and by the middle of the 20th century, it gained independence and maintained the kind of western government structure left behind. Yet by mid-1970, a tyrant named Amin basically screwed up the whole country and Uganda became an impoverished land, much like its neighbors. After this guy was ousted and went into exile, Uganda was bombarded by a civil war with a cult called "The Lord's Resistance Army" that caused constant threat up in the north. Lately, the battles with this gang had subsided and the country had been slowly picking up the pieces at a snail pace. However, it has maintained a relatively stable political, religious, social, and economical progression compared to other African countries. In short, Uganda had a shot in achieving a bright future for the future generations.

The book was highly enjoyable, and I honestly admired some of the beautiful natural scenery captured in the centerfold. The entire piece of literature was pretty comprehensive too. But of course, it didn't mention anything about orphanages or medical clinics in the rural areas.

The next item on the checklist was to gather all the supplies I could get from any generous donors. Soap, shampoo, wet wipes, tums, cough medicine, vinyl gloves, story books, crayons, paper, candy, and all other hygiene and school supplies you could think of would be helpful for the community, children and adults alike. It was the first time I saw hundreds of toothpastes filled up an army-size duffle bag, and it was kind of fun trying to squeeze all the donations you could pack into a bag within the weight limit for check-in purposes. I hope none of these would go wasted.

Actually, it wasn't even enough, I later discovered.

Time flied by very quickly, and the date for the second and final meeting had arrived. It was *the* time to find out who will do what precisely, on which day, and how to accomplish some of the objectives listed on the trip description.

We met at the FCA center in Modesto, seated in a conference room, and acted a little more serious than the previous meeting. Since most team members were newbies and only Doctor Doug and Raeanne could formally handle the medical part, each of us was assigned an internal role to start with. I was the camcorder man and the assistant treasurer. No sweat.

Next, the lesson plan. Wait- what? No prior communications had ever mentioned anything about teaching in any capacity. Yet apparently, I was the only one out of the loop. Most people instinctively picked up from Arlene a packet of materials with instructions in it. I had no idea how I would be able to fit into this role, given that I had never taught before. So I passed.

I had to admit that subsequently, on the one hand my passivity was a mistake and I did regret for not picking up this task. It was a great way to build relationships with the children and it wasn't rocket science anyway.

On the other hand, in hindsight God had a unique plate designated for each one of us, and I could not say for sure that things would have been absolutely better had I chosen to teach.

The discussion then switched to some of the administrative topics that did not truly pertain to me, so I pretended to listen and thought about the preparations I needed to make to fulfill my roles.

The final item for discussion was about the supplies we needed to bring. It seemed we had planned too much on the "core" materials, such as medicine and art & crafts supplies, and forgot about the resources we would need to network with the orphans for the entertainment / recreational part of the interaction.

"We can slip a few frisbees in one of the bags. We really don't have much room left in any of the luggage" suggested Shirley.

Frisbees? What the heck?! I did not hide my raised eyebrow.

"Umm… what about some soccer balls? I understand that frisbees would be easier to bring, but soccer is like the international language in sport. I don't think the kids would know how to play frisbees, and we can flatten the balls and bring some small pumps and needles." I thought I made a clear statement.

"So? They can learn!" shouted Shirley, all the way across the room with certitude.

"*Oh crap.*" I murmured to myself.

Later, I convinced Bob to flatten a few soccer balls and bring them along with a couple sets of pumps and needles. I told him that we could give the children "a choice" in case they didn't know how to play with a frisbee. I was very insistent on this issue and determined to exercise some civil disobedience, and Bob was okay with that.

Well, at least we had made some good progress and had gradually finalized on the schedule, projects that needed to be done, and some proper expectations. As the big day approached, I took a couple of extra days off to quiet down, relax, and switched my focus to think about the girls that I liked.

Was I prepared? Yes and no, I figured. On the one hand, I read a lot about Uganda and world missions, and I knew I would be working with people that I may not like. But on the other hand, impromptu skills, or the lack of, could make a whole lot of differences in some situations while traveling overseas, and I couldn't say that I still have a lot of those in inventory after having worked in a large corporation for a couple of years.

I sensed that I couldn't rely on my teammates, or even myself anymore. All I had left to trust was just God and Him alone.

A few days before takeoff, a call from a FCA staff basically threw off a good chunk of what everyone had already prepared for.

"Hello?"

"Oh hi, is this Ambrose? This is Tori from FCA. I am the one helping Arlene on some of the administrative things for the Uganda trip, remember?"

"Oh yeah Tori, what's up?" I also remember that Tori was Bob's fiancé, "Any news for me?"

"Yes...hmm...I just want to let you know that someone from the team had decided not to go at the last minute, but the team is still going. I am not too sure about the details and as of now, we don't know what the impact would be. But the trip is definitely still on as scheduled."

"Who is that?" (*Come on Tori, give me some good news!*)

"Don, the leader. You haven't met him yet, and Arlene will take over his position."

Ha! The leader ditched at the last moment! Who could have thought of that?!

---

*Al Bundy was the protagonist in a sitcom called "Married... with Children" that was broadcasted from the late 80s to the late 90s. Al worked a shoe salesman and his biggest achievement in life was making four touchdowns in a single football game back in high school.

From Sympathy (pseudo) To Empathy

Ambrose Tse

Chapter 02: 50 Hours

You guessed it- that was how long it took to get to the final destination from SFO.

Since Tori hung up, I wasn't all that freaked out. I knew I probably should, but it was weird that I didn't. I wasn't even emotional. If the team would need to figure its way out in Uganda, then so be it. If there were any road blocks waiting ahead, God will provide and our experiences would only make us stronger.

If we could come back alive, that was. And this was not an exaggeration at all.

Perhaps I needed to thank my former boss who give me the motivation to make the above declaration.

****

"Ambrose, you heard what happened to Betsy, right?" Jim asked calmly after calling me into his office for a one-on-one dialogue. This happened at the beginning of April 2003.

"Yeah, she had been saying that she wanted to move on. But I guessed it was an abrupt announcement for everyone." Carefully choosing my words, a seamless transition or digression seemed to be the best approach, especially it was obvious that Jim was about to lose his temper.

"I am okay with her departure. It was good that she found what she wanted. The only thing was that I will be two people short for awhile, with your two-week vacation coming up." My immediate supervisor looked at me in the eye and still sounded a little overwhelmed.

Intimidated by his tone (I was a naïve, innocent boy back then) and not knowing what the conversation was heading to, I

27

couldn't help but to become defensive: "Oh, I am sure it's easy to find a replacement. Besides, I have already signed up for that two-week slot a long time ago. It was for a good cause too, you know, helping the hungry and dying children in Africa."

"I DON'T CARE ABOUT THE HUNGRY OR DYING CHILDREN IN AFRICA!" Jim roared back like a lion.

My eyes were wide opened, absolutely shocked.

"Oh, okay…" Easing the tension with a soft tone and acting like an obedient little child, I pretended to understand his point of view and nodded while my blood was boiling.

The psychopath then switched topics to work flow scheduling for the next couple of months, which audit to add onto the backlog, Betsy's crappy attitude since she was hired, and finally discussed about the tentative audits that will be assigned to me once I returned after the trip. Before I stepped out of his room, the weasel commended: "Don't tell anyone I said *that*, okay?"

"Oh, sure, absolutely. No problem, I promised." I smiled back, blood still boiling.

****

Later, we found out that Don was asked to be in charge of a fund-raising project for his organization as soon as he returned from the Dominican Republic, so reportedly he **had** to ditch. I wondered what might have actually happened between them and FCA though.

Just a random thought, of course; this is something I would never be able to find out.

Everyone was already at SFO and checked in by the time I showed up on the most important day of that month. It was an early Wednesday evening, so checking in was smooth and there was plenty of time before boarding. Some people from church came to see me off, and my family also made it just in time. We were supposed to first fly out to London, take an 8 hour lay-over at Heathrow, and continue onto Entebbe, Uganda, to arrive at the crack of dawn of the following day.

"Wow, you have lots of supporting friends." Bob commented.

"Yeah, some really came out of their way." I responded politely and positively as we were all waiting in line to board, felt a little embarrassed for being late and making myself appeared out-group.

The flight was pretty full, and the travel agency appeared to have done the best it could to make the team seated somewhat together. Fortunately, Bob, the next youngest guy on the team, was sitting right next to me, and we were making some small talk- some rapport that seemed to be missing since we met.

The 10-hour flight to London was quick, but the following 8 hours of lay over wasn't.

The mini shopping mall inside Heathrow was quite remarkable, but I doubted if anyone could even spend more than a few hours being entertained in that glamorous confinement. After awhile, I sat down on a bench in front of a gift shop, and Pastor Mick joined me. Shortly, he took out a guitar and started playing and singing- so loud that people could hear him from a mile away.

Boy, did that feel odd, especially inside an airport. But hey, guess what? No one stopped him, so I guessed it was okay after all.

I decided to get back on my feet and continued to wander in circles, trying to find a teammate that I could socialize with. To my dismay, none of them was around until about an hour before the connecting flight departed at the gate. Everyone looked tired and was speechless just like me. I knocked myself out after claiming my seat, too exhausted to even want to enjoy some of the fancy features offered on the plane.

****

A strong, bright orange ray of sunshine immediately blinded my sight the moment I stepped out of the aircraft. It was about 6 o'clock in the morning, and after about 30 hours of flying and waiting, our team had finally arrived at Entebbe, Uganda. I wasn't too thrilled at that time, thanks to the overwhelming fatigue and jetlag, and knowing that there would be a full plate waiting ahead.

We were greeted by our hosts Will, Liz, and her sister, who worked at the airport, and praised God in a circle for His protection after retrieving all of our luggage. The airport reminded me of the old Kai Tek Airport of Hong Kong in the 1980's, especially the color and monotone design of the walls and flooring. We quickly headed to the car park, which appeared to be systematically and sophisticatedly constructed. Two 14-passenger vans, the chauffeurs, and Will's car were waiting for us to load the bags. Suddenly, the sky turned dark and it started to pour cats and dogs within a fraction of a second. I was badly soaked, and continued to load the luggage in one of the vans as fast as I could. The scene was fairly dramatic in a corny way, but I could only interpret the sudden shower as a cozy welcome. Plus, it helped to cool things down a bit in case it got too hot later during the day. Subsequently, I remembered reading that April was still in the middle of Uganda's rainy season, and it rained almost every single day while we were there.

The rain only lasted for 10 minutes, but it felt like someone was pouring buckets of water just for the heck of it. We stopped by a bank in flamboyant downtown to exchange some cold hard cash in Kampala, Uganda's capital. After that, the vehicles streamed through different parts of town, from the noisy marketplace occupied by street vendors and women carrying their belongings in a basket on top of their heads, to the busy streets where no cars would ever yield or stop to any other cars or pedestrians, and finally to a quiet restaurant up on a hill.

The restaurant was a haven compared to the hustle and bustle only moments ago. Even though the food selection was limited and tasted pretty bland (some hardboiled eggs, bread, steamed and mashed plantain as known as "matoke", and other premature fruits), the place did give a fair view of the capital's landscape. Short buildings were scattered in sprawls, and the pale brownish green mountains from the far side made up most of the scenery. There were huts, too, in the middle of nowhere and few shops operating next to each other here and there. Most roads, like the rest of Africa, were not paved, so dust and sand would literally flare up even when a bike passed by. In general and with all due respect, I failed to see much organization in city planning.

Breakfast took more than an hour for no apparent reason. We then made our way to the next stop, which was a wholesale medical supply distributor named JMS (or "Joint Medical Store"), to see what was available there and what Doctor Doug could get if he needed anything. I was lucky enough to have claimed the shotgun seat of the van throughout the entire ride, next to the quiet chauffeur, and capitalized on the opportunity to take some pictures and videos from the passenger side of the window.

A problem started to surface after awhile: rush hour appeared to be constant, and the traffic condition was comparable to that of Ho Chi Minh City in Vietnam. Bikes, mopeds, cars, trucks, cows, and anything that moved were all fighting to crawl on the main roads, inch by inch, as if everyone was racing at a Formula One competition. All the drivers looked super aggressive, and the space between each vehicle was no more than half a foot, at the very most.

31

"What are you doing with that camcorder?!" the frown from the passengers of the vehicles nearby instructed me to stop, and so did my headache from the honking and sudden braking and turning controlled by Mr. Chauffeur.

I put the machine down, gathered my composure, and tried to see what else I could do by being aloof in the front next to the driver.

It didn't look like Mr. Chauffeur could speak English. I didn't recall if he even said "hello" or nodded. But that would be strange, since Uganda used to be a British colony. Maybe he was a quiet person?

-Phew-

"What the…?!"

Mr. Chauffeur suddenly threw an empty water bottle out the window after he took the last drip, slurred out a long and coarse expression in the local dialect, and sped up with a long honk.

Oh God, am I going to be stuck with this guy for the rest of the ride? I don't want to get shot!

Strange enough, there was no retaliation from the other drivers. Not even a middle finger. And the bumpy ride continued with the usual braking and honking.

After another hour or so, we made it safe and sound to JMS. The majority of the team was patiently waiting at an outdoor cafeteria after a 5-minute tour, while Doctor Doug and Arlene went inside for their serious shopping business.

"Do you have any idea how long this is going to take?" I asked one of the ladies from our team.

"No, I don't even know why we are here. I thought we were all going to Dorcas once we landed. They must need to buy something".

"I see." Of course, I couldn't see how they could buy anything without the money I just exchanged, which were all in my wallet. Or were they just window shopping?

The sun was shining nice and bright after that 10-minute shower in the early morning, and we each bought ourselves a bottle of ice water from the mini snack shop. The ladies gathered themselves around a couple of tables and talked. A few of us were just pointlessly walking around, browsing at the surrounding landscape. Mr. Chauffeur was sitting and waiting at a table in the corner by himself, eyes closed and right palm on the top of his head.

His miserable, exhausted look could no way be associated with the aggression on his face from only minutes ago. The picture looked quite odd to me. I bought another bottle of water and handed it over to him. Before I could decide what to say to him, he actually saw me coming and reached out his hands with a big smile and said "thank you" in a soft tone. I smiled back, but couldn't quite connect the dots. What might have caused his mood swing? I meant, that small act of kindness couldn't be that powerful, right? And for the longest time I assumed he couldn't speak any English!

About another hour or so, Doctor Doug and Arlene came back out empty handed, and announced that they would need to know what the doctors in the clinic needed before they could buy any supplies.

"*Oh, really?*" I didn't even bother to roll my eyes.

We rode for another 2 hours heading northeast towards Mbale, the third largest town of Uganda, before our butts started to get numb. We left behind the driving excitement before we realized it, and Mother Nature made up the majority of our scenic view for the remainder of the ride.

"Will asked us if we need to stop for lunch. Does anyone want food?" Arlene related the message as both vehicles stopped after we passed Jinja, Uganda's second largest town where the Nile River began to flow. Most of us shook our heads, but told her that we needed a 15-minute stretching break.

Will was a quiet, gentle guy and a great host. He tried to accommodate us and talk to each of us, although he was reportedly pretty tired from driving to the airport to pick us up from the night before. His wife Liz was a very straightforward person, but you would still feel comfortable asking her any questions.

"Hey, you guys want to get going?" Someone yelled after 5 minutes into the break.

"Huh?"

"I mean, we shouldn't stay here too long."

"Why not?"

"Will told us that there could be some snakes around, probably not a python though."

The bright side was that we had the next several days to get to know each other better. And we did.

Running away too soon from potentially bitten by a poisonous reptile only helped made the limbs became stiff again sooner than before. Damn it, it was worse than being in a 14-hour flight because you couldn't even stand up in a car for more than a few seconds, if at all possible. I took my camcorder out again, hoping to divert my attention and catch some candid moments of rural Uganda.

Thanks to Mr. Chauffeur, he slowed down each time I held up the machine, trying to lend me a hand. I actually preferred him to just keep driving normally, or else we would be on this commute forever. I was still grateful for his help, and it was a good deal made for a bottle of water worth about 30 cents.

After another 2 hours we've reached Mbale, our last stop for anything we wanted to get before heading to Dorcas. I personally believed, nonetheless, the last thing the team needed was another stop! *Geez, who needed another stop? Who planned all this? Haven't we been on the road for more than 48 hours already? Can we just go to Dorcas and settle down?* As soon as Mr. Chauffeur turned the ignition off, I couldn't help but to jump out from the van and headed to the streets alone. My frustration subsided pretty quickly when I immediately noticed all the attention I got from the curious local people. I must have looked unexplainably funny. But I wasn't exactly intimidated; I couldn't allow myself to even feel uncomfortable, or else I would have to do so for the rest of my time here in Uganda.

A child with a puzzled look walked by slowly and tried to figure who I was and what the heck I was doing in his 'hood. Oh, I meant *her* 'hood- most of the teenage boys and girls I met had very short haircut.

"Hi, how are you? What is your name?" I engaged slowly with my signature cute, chubby smile.

"….?"

Okay, let's try this again; the zealous enthusiasm from a stranger might have scared her. But hey, it was my first conversation with a local!

"…"

Nothing changed.

35

"Emanruoysitahwdeksaeh?" A deep, coarse voice suddenly emerged from behind. Yes, it was Mr. Chauffeur who came to the rescue!

"Halifa."

"Her name is Halifa." The deep, coarse voice translated.

Knowing that a meaningful dialogue probably won't take place, I took some candy out from my bag and handed over to her.

"Uoyrofydnacemoss'ereh."

"Monyala." The soft voice replied.

"You are welcome." I put my smile back on. It wasn't hard to figure out what "Monyala" meant.

This first encounter was by far the most refreshing experience within the last 48 hours.

The sun started to hide behind the clouds during the early evening hours. In less than an hour we'll be arriving at the guesthouse next to Dorcas. Excited?! Kind of. Worried? Heck yeah! We, or the team leader, had not figured out where we will be sleeping tonight, and the places we passed by in the rural area were anything but impressive. How come they look so different from the pictures in the $20 guidebook I bought from Borders?

Well, ready or not here comes the children, yelling and running around behind the fences. We've arrived at Dorcas Orphanage.

From Sympathy (pseudo) To Empathy

Chapter 03: Ready? Set... Cry!

Warning: For the rest of this book, please exercise extreme cautions when reading through the events and experiences described. The author cannot be held responsible for consequences caused by any emotional upheaval, which includes but not limited to upset stomach, teary eyes, gnashing of teeth, and aggressive behavior after knowing that you have just spent your hard-earned money on a "childish" story.

****

"The children have been waiting and wanting to give us a welcome ceremony", announced Arlene, "but it was getting late, so we'll have them perform for us tomorrow instead".

"Where are we staying tonight?" asked one of the ladies.

"Well, Liz and I have talked about this, and it seems like the best place would be the guesthouse nearby."

"Is a guesthouse like a hotel or something?" I quietly asked one of the ladies standing next to me.

"I am not sure. But it's probably a little different than a hotel, or even a hostel."

I later found out what a guesthouse was like. No, it was not anything like a hotel, motel, or a hostel. It had a bed in the room, but all other facilities were shared. It was a pretty common and wholesome accommodation on the continent, a notch above tents and huts.

"But the children still wanted to welcome us by presenting a song, and we can tour the children center a bit." Arlene announced again.

After Mr. Chauffeur dropped our bags off and returned to Kampala, we headed over to the "Dorcas Children Center"- which was a more appropriate appellation- that served not only orphans but any children that showed up. In fact, children and adults could hang out there if they wanted, and it also functioned as a community center. Things like this just weren't as clearly defined or classified here in Africa. In addition, they didn't want to make any kids feel worse than the situation they were practically in by calling it an "orphanage".

Before all of us arrived at the gate, we saw from a distance over 30 children, all wearing sharp, bright, and torn clothing, rushed to the front, organized themselves, and began singing and clapping with surprisingly robust enthusiasm. The performance had been repeatedly rehearsed, apparently.

While the team was standing a few feet away enjoying the noises made, I took my camcorder out to capture the show, and flashes from a few other cameras were also all over the place.

It was indeed fun watching these kids sing, but the first thing that caught my attention was their feet. No shoes? How come? Not even a pair of sandals? Each of them got mud all over their feet and all the way up to their knees. The fading skin pigment, blisters, callus, open pores, and cracks on their feet made it difficult to tell what their feet really looked like. I could imagine that it was going to hurt if they walk on the dusty roads barefooted. And how about all the animals and insects that crawled on the ground?

Before I could figure out the answers to all these questions, the kids finished singing and some swiftly returned to the center. Several other smaller, younger children remained standing in the front and we went up to greet them. From the recent experience with Halifa, I know I couldn't expect much. I smiled, thanked them for their hospitality, and padded them on their heads. That was the time when I suddenly felt a little odd.

I couldn't readily define or verbalize what the realization was. Things just weren't supposed to be the way it should. My excitement vanished since deplaning, but it wasn't because of the exhaustion from hours of traveling. When Tori told me over the phone that the leader ditched, I wasn't all that freak out about the uncertainty ahead. But when I started to breathe the air of Uganda into my lungs, and when I saw and interacted with the quiet local people, heard the noises from their marketplace, tasted a little bit of their food during breakfast, shook their hands, felt their emotions- I got lost.

After all the kids turned around and went back behind the gate, Arlene announced that it was getting too late and dark to tour the center according to Liz. So we proceeded to the medical clinic. The clinic's official name was "Shared Blessings Center".

By the way, I forgot to mention: Dorcas Children Center was founded by Liz. It all began one day when she picked up an abandoned child on the street. From that time on, she started to pick up more hungry, dying, and thrown away kids, and other people brought their children to her. A child care center gradually evolved and caught the attention of FCA, whom subsidized the small organization. As hundred of kids began to gather, Dorcas reportedly became a landmark in the neighborhood. Liz sure had a big heart, and the physicality to embody that.

"Lalalalalalalalalalalalalalalalalalalalala!!!!!!!!!!"

A lady in a light green uniform suddenly sprinted out from nowhere with her hands widespread in the air, just when the team stepped onto the clinic's turf. She was singing and screaming on top of her lungs at the same time- obviously another "welcome song".

Wow, that was dramatic. With all that energy I thought she was going to pick one of us up and throw that person halfway in the air!

41

The rest of the staff, which were just one doctor and a couple of nurses on duty, walked out from the clinic and greeted us like how we expected. Jacqueline, the nurse with the vocal gift, continued to "sing" and shook each of our hands. Some of us gave her a big smile, either out of courtesy or being amused by such vigor.

A chicken blocked our way to safeguard its territory, a corrugated box hiding in the corner behind the receptionist desk, as we treaded slowly into the clinic. We proceeded slowly to the waiting area, which was surprisingly peaceful and rather empty, as the sun slowly sets. A few patients were sitting on a bench, completely subdued with their heads slightly tilted downward and eyes closed. A silly but scary thought flashed in my mind: did they already die while waiting for diagnosis?

The staff escorted us to a bigger room, and we were finally exposed to the harsh reality for the very first time. More than half a dozen beds, some rusted, broken and taped, were all occupied by various patients: pregnant women, injured young men, crippled kids, some with open bloody wounds, the malnourished with bones literally sticking out from their joints but covered by their thick skin, and...you can visualize the rest, if you really wanted to.

There was no crying, panicking, or wailing. In fact, it was as quiet as my office at 6 o'clock in the evening on any given day in downtown San Francisco. The smell of the mixture of blood, medicine, and mud in the air however reminded me that I was in Africa.

"Is it okay for us to just come in like this?" I wondered. Apparently, our invasion of privacy was not a priority concern for the ill.

None of the team members said anything nor asked any questions. The doctor detected the odd silence fairly quickly, so he showed us some of his and hi-tech medical equipment.

"Hey! Is that a Bunsen burner?" I noticed something familiar when we were directed to the doctor's office.

I moved up and took a closer look at the burner, along with a telescope and a few Petri dishes. Last time I saw them was in my high school classes. Those were exactly the same gears used for my biology and chemistry labs.

"Yes, I used them to analyze my patients' cases." The young doctor spotted my undivided attention, and explained with a proud smile on his face.

"Oh... I see." I nodded with an educated facial expression, diligently hiding my shock.

Without further ado, we were taken to the guesthouse, which was Will and Liz's home with several extra rooms at the back reserved for guests. As soon as we finished touring the clinic, we were asked to stay there for the rest of the trip. Pastor Mick, Bob, and I were sharing a room while Doctor Doug and John became roommates in another room. Four other bedrooms, each with an individual bathroom inside, were divided among the seven ladies. Since Arlene was the team leader, she got her own room.

Let's take a few moments to describe the internal layout of the compound and the surrounding environment: Will's house was at the front, and the large backyard served as a common area connected to a gated side entrance on the left and the men's bedrooms on the right, with a bathroom in between. Behind the backyard was another short building, or so-call the main guesthouse building, with the four ladies' bedrooms at each corner and a common dining area in the middle. Behind this guesthouse was a short path leading to a gazebo. The whole premise was either fenced or gated. Will explained that occasionally he could hear different animals growl in the middle of the night. Needless to say, Will and Liz were loaded in the 'hood, presumably thanks to its partnership with FCA.

For the purposes of our missions, actually, we couldn't have asked for better: a 5-minute walk on the muddy road after you turned left from the guesthouse would lead you to a split path, with Dorcas on the right and the clinic on the left. The distance between Dorcas and the clinic was less than 200 feet away. The commute to work was quite pleasant at times when the 3 locations formed a decent isosceles triangle. It would be almost impossible for any newcomers to get lost during the daytime.

A 5-minute drive to Sironko, the closest town, would enable us to buy trivia supplements like sodas and phone cards. For internet access, we would need to go back to Mbale and visit one of the "internet cafes", or small businesses with rows of desktop computer that served no drinks.

One pleasant surprise that nobody in the team had ever dreamt about was a couple of young folks from the UK that had volunteered to help Liz out for about a month at Dorcas. Mark was a tall, skinny, handsome, and quiet guy; and Jonathan was funny and talkative. They were both in their early 20's like me.

By the way, nobody was really sure about the mission anymore since the ditching news of our leader was released.

"Okay...since tomorrow is a Saturday and more kids will show up, I think we can do a worship program in the morning. After that, they will finish up with the welcoming ceremony." Arlene the new CEO announced.

What? That wasn't it? The songs they just sang were longer than 10minutes already! I was beyond dumbfounded.

"We had a long day today, so let's do a little bit of the coordination and rundown for the worship program tomorrow after breakfast." Pastor Mick interjected.

A feast was cooked up during our tour time and we were served lavishly with fresh fruits, cooked vegetables, chicken, and the famous matoke (a must have traditional, fulfilling Ugandan dish at every meal, just like bread in France). I didn't realize how famished I was until the aroma of the food simmered into the air. I couldn't have felt more blessed.

Because our bedroom was so small, Pastor Mick, Bob, and I had to unpack our bags and only take in the mandatory personal items, such as toiletry, clothing, and some reading materials. There was a bunk bed, a twin-size bed, and an old fan standing between the beds in the room. Pastor Mick said that he preferred the twin size bed, and Bob took the bottom bunk bed.

It wasn't until after I climbed up to my comfort zone and fixed the bedding did I realize a few other guests were waiting to say hello. Three of them, presumably parents and child, quiet but active, stayed at the corner of the walls and ceiling, each raised one of their legs and waved.

"Oh God, look what we've got here?" I heaved a sigh, "At least they are not spiders or cockroaches." I self-consoled.

The mosquito family refused to move, until the intruder (me, of course) swung a paper notebook and drove them out through the window after 5 minutes of intense chasing and smacking.

"It looks like we would need to close the window for the rest of the night." One of the roommates proposed.

"But what if it gets too warm?" I brainstormed out loud.

"The fan isn't working." Bob answered after checking the antique when Will showed us how to turn it on earlier.

"We will just have to see. But we can't afford to let the mosquitoes bite us and make us sick." Pastor Mick made a good point.

Bob went out and came back a few minutes later with 3 bottles of coke. "Look what I've got from the fridge." He was like a soldier who came back after stealing a top secret from the enemy.

All 3 of us gave a toast and finished the refreshment in no time.

"Pastor Mick", I asked, "What is a good book to read in the Bible at this time?"

Without any hesitation, he said "1ˢᵗ Peter. Why don't you start from chapter one and read it aloud for us?"

I flipped to that page, took a deep breath, and began reading.

"...*blessed be the God and Father of our Lord Jesus Christ! By his great mercy he gave us new birth into a living hope through the resurrection of Jesus Christ from the dead, that is, into an inheritance imperishable, undefiled, and unfading. It is reserved in heaven for you, who by God's power are protected through faith for a salvation ready to be revealed in the last time. This brings you great joy, although you may have to suffer for a short time in various trials. Such trials show the proven character of your faith, which is much more valuable than gold – gold that is tested by fire, even though it is passing away– and will bring praise and glory and honor when Jesus Christ is revealed. You have not seen him, but you love him. You do not see him now but you believe in him, and so you rejoice with an indescribable and glorious joy, because you are attaining the goal of your faith – the salvation of your souls...*"

By verse 9 my voice started to tremble, lost control of the pitch, and got hysterical and cried like a big baby. I stopped right at the end of chapter one and gasped to calm myself down.

Pastor Mick reacted immediately and prayed for humility, protection, and surrendering control. A few moments of silence after saying amen, we decided to turn the lights off. Before I lost consciousness, I kept asking myself: "What the hell am I doing here?"

****

Several hours later I regained consciousness and felt a cool breeze blowing from my right-hand side. No, it wasn't a dream. Didn't we close the window before going to bed? Or, maybe it was too stuffy that someone opened it at the risk of inviting more mosquitoes? I was still too tired to sit up, so I just hoped that I could go back to sleep as soon as possible and not having to worry. As I wiped the saliva at the corner of my mouth with the sleeves, a loud and low clamor suddenly squeaked through the darkness. Wait- it was more like a screech that changed to a yelp.

Oh crap.

Whatever that was, my fatigue vanished and I was holding my breath. Was it from a snake nearby? Or a lizard? Or both? Should I just play dead so the creature would ignore me? God, I thought we were secured in a gated area! What should I do now? Turn the lights on, wake everyone up, and hunt down the creature(s)? What if I were wrong? I meant, what if it was just some beasts howling from a distance? Man, I was overwhelmingly confused.

As the "noises" die down, I recaptured my breath and decided to hide like an ostrich. Before my eyelids dropped all the way down, a series of rhythm disclosed its original sources:

gugugugu ahahahah bobobobo...ahahahah bobobobo gugugugu... bobobobo gugugugu ahahahah...

It was Pastor Mick!

47

And he is also a magician! I am not saying that he acted like a clown or an acrobat working in a circus, but what he did was nothing less than a performer who walked on a big yoga ball, threw and caught three bottles in the air, and played hula hoop all at the same time. Personally, his amazing skills should be qualified for the Guinness Book of World of Records. But if I suggested that to him, he might sit on me and give me the *"bobobobo"*.

With all due respect, I wasn't being vulgar. Hey, I did the same stuff too, just not all simultaneously. My mom repeatedly told me that my snoring worried her a lot, and sometimes I talked in sleep too (that was what I was told). The third attribute? Well, I could be a creative composer, but only privately. Pastor Mick's "music" was a little monotonous.

The zephyr had no aroma and no temperature. I put a blanket delicately on my face, wrapped it around tightly on my body, rolled to the left-hand side, and returned to sleep in no time.

Thanks be to God.

Chapter 04: Taste of Uganda

I woke up next morning still feeling tired and perplexed, but was probably better than had I not cried out like a freak. Moving on with life, I robotically brushed up, changed, and went to the family room for breakfast.

Breakfast was another lavish meal by local standard. There were passion fruit juice, tea, and coffee, along with some bread, millets, and fresh fruits laid out on the table in buffet style. I picked up a tall steel bottle of hot milk, opened the cap, and looked into the steam.

"Wow, this is fresh! It smelled like it was just milked from a cow minutes ago!" I was pleasantly surprised by the new find.

"I believe this was milked from one of the goats in the back." One of the ladies answered in a low voice.

I poured out a quarter of a small cup and took a sip of the good, fresh stuff from Mother Nature, ignoring my slight lactose intolerance. The milk was too good to be true! It was nothing like those half gallon cartons that sat for ages in the supermarket fridge.

"Hmm... I wonder where did they pasteurize the milk?" I tried to get a more sophisticated answer from the crowd.

Dead silence.

My stomach showed me the brutal answer within minutes.

Allison was generous enough to let me use the toilet in her room when I secretly asked for her permission as soon as breakfast time was over. I was not going to take a chance with the squatty-potty in the men's bathroom if it came out watery and splash some on my pants.

Beat beat beat beat beat, beat beat! Bratttt!!!

"Haaaaaaaaa!!!!!!!" I couldn't even wait for the chill to subside to express my satisfying relief. The symphony was no less entertaining than the one orchestrated by Pastor Mick several hours ago!

Nothing substantial came out. That was good, I thought, failing to remember what a diarrhea should look like.

A meeting was about to start in a few minutes. I quickly wrapped up and came to this critical moment to test my newly acquired skill: flushing the toilet effectively.

The rule observed was: if there were no water at all, all I needed to do was to put the lid down and put a note on top of it. But it was only a few moments after breakfast, so I assumed water should still be available. I slowly tapped on the handle, and pressed all the way down as soon a small water stream flowing into the bowl. There was no guarantee if there would be enough water to flush again, so everything had to go down in one shot.

Gush....dadadadada....goutgoutgout...

Ha, ha, ha; surprisingly perfect. The semi-creamy bowl of café au lait with extra splashes of caramel went down in one gulp. There was hardly a trace of toilet paper left neither.

I turned around and washed my hands. After I turned the faucet on, water slowly dripped and stopped after a couple of seconds.

"Oh crap! This can't be true! I just had more than enough water to flush the toilet!" I yelled quietly in frustration.

No matter how I stuck my fingers into or creatively played with the faucet, there was no miracle. I looked at my right palm and shook my head. The width of the local toilet paper roll was only half of what it was back home.

What should I do? What should I do?

The best bet was to go to another toilet and try the faucet there, and I would need to act fast and find an unoccupied one while the aroma of my fresh production diffused in air.

I sneaked out and found a glowing lifesaver immediately. Someone put a big bottle of hand sanitizer on top of the fridge!

"Isn't this even better?" The light bulb on top of my head was shining bright and clear.

I squeezed a small puddle of the alcohol on my right palm and used my left index figure to rub the liquid in circles. The sanitizer was strong and comforting, although it felt weird that on one hand you have some powerful detox cleaner, and on the other hand the sanitizer is mixed with your own crap. I slightly prayed that all the smell would quickly vaporize and everything would return to normal.

After shaking my wrists and swinging my arms several times to get the sanitizer to dry quicker, I walked towards the backyard and acted confidently. It looked like though it will take awhile for my hands to become completely dry. Meanwhile, a group of people had already sat down in the gazebo and Will waved at me.

I jogged quickly towards him, where most of my teammates and a few young strangers were already chatting. Will introduced them as the day doctors from the clinic. The one that looked like Michael Jordan was Roger, the more innocuous-looking one was Sidney, and the third doctor who looked cautious and somewhat introverted called himself Godfrey.

Before I could react, each of them shook my hand passionately. When I reached out my left hand and tried to gently pull their right palms away, they also stretched out their left hands and shook the back of my right hand even harder.

I have never, in my life, felt so bad before.

"Are you alright?" Bob asked. Perhaps I did look a little uneasy.

"Ah- no, I had a stomachache and went to the bathroom right after breakfast." Smiling embarrassingly.

"Is it diarrhea or just crap?"

"I think it was just... crap." I confessed while looking down at my hands. Fortunately, Bob stopped asking.

Will told us briefly about how the doctors worked and coordinated with each other at the clinic, and our new acquaintances went back soon after his introduction. I really appreciated how they all left the clinic and came to meet us, even just for a short period of time.

Pastor Mick took over and talked about the worship rundown. He picked several simple and happy songs that would appeal to pre-teen children, and started tuning the guitar. Apparently, those songs were far too difficult for me.

Wait- it was going to be my first time participating in a worship team. What am I supposed to do? Clap? Sing along? Or just smile and do everything else a few seconds slower than the rest of the team? Hey you know what- that's all good; I could make a fool of myself anywhere, as long as nobody knows me there!

We were ready to go after Pastor Mick spent 20 minutes on the run down, taught all of us the hand signals, facial expressions, and when to do what. "We" referred to Bob, Denise, Brenda, Allison, and myself. Doctor Doug, RaeAnne, Arlene, and the older folks were either preparing to operate in the clinic or meeting with someone somewhere about something.

Alright!! Let's get the ball rolling and start to rummmmbbbbllleeee!!!!!

****

Everything was a rendezvous again: as soon as the children saw us approaching to the front gate of the center, they all rushed out and shook our hands. No singing this time though, but our little friends just wanted to touch us somehow, if they couldn't fight their way in for a decent, rough handshake.

John, Doctor Doug, and I were standing side by side and we all noticed just how much mud, and perhaps some other unknown stuff, were on each of their tiny hands.

"When do you guys think they last washed their hands?" John uttered quietly through his teeth.

"Just don't stick your hand into your month." Doctor Doug kept his eyes and ears opened and kept shaking the kids' hands with a friendly smile.

I couldn't agree more.

When all the hassle and commotion finally settled down and the kids returned to their turf, at the corner of my left eye I caught a glimpse of someone sitting under a tree with his head bowed down. I made a signal to Bob and both of us walked towards that boy. The boy didn't seem to notice that we were walking towards him. His head continued to tilt downwards and eyes closed. For a moment I though he was either asleep or half alive like those at the clinic the evening before, but obviously that was me being overly sensitive and irrational again.

The boy showed some responses when we were only a few feet apart. And as soon as he rubbed his eyes with the back of his hands, Bob and I understood why he was not part of the group.

He wasn't crippled or whatnot. Both pupils in his eyes were mostly white like glue.

Pastor Mick and some other locals joined us and try to greet this poor little fellow while I was still hesitating on what to say or do. In our frivolous effort we all tried to say something, but like many younger ones he did not understand English. He uttered something back that sounded like he was excited, so we padded and grabbed his arms to make him feel better. Will saw the little crowd from several feet away and gave us a hand.

"His name is Sam, and he can't see." Will reported to us after exchanging a conversation with Sam. "None of the boys here really know where he is from, because no one played with him. But we can find out more."

"Is there any way we can have an eye doctor to take a look at his case?" asked one of the men.

"We'll have to first find out if he is alone (or "orphaned"). If he has a parent, then we'll let that person take charge. Otherwise, there is not much we can do here." replied Will.

"There is no eye doctor around?" I asked.

"No, the closest hospital is in Mbale, and I don't think they have an eye doctor there either. We'll see."

Damn right we can see. But Sam can't. What's the problem here? In anguish I totally couldn't comprehend the situation at all.

We had to move on to the worship. We invited Sam to come along, and each of us gave him a little touch and talked to him. He was smiling frantically as if he had not interacted with anyone for years.

I was holding my tears in. Hard.

****

Hey, is that Beyonce there?!

I switched my focus to someone else that caught my attention. Don't get me wrong here- I was not hallucinating. I did see a mini Beyonce: the way she moved, danced, and played with her peers. All in a miniature form.

And no, I wasn't ogling her. I was trying to say that it was kind of cool to see a girl at the age of 6 or 7, at the most, to be able to casually perform like some of the pros you see on TV. Trust me, she had all the attributes to become a red hot celebrity. If she were in Hollywood, I can bet you anything that she will become a superstar.

But she was at Dorcas.

The worship team found a muddy area between a wall and a bunch of broken chairs to use as the performing stage. My stomach was acting up again as we were setting things up. I took off and tried to find a bathroom somewhere inside the children center. More children greeted me and shook my hands as I was wandering around. They all seemed to be unreasonably excited- perhaps they have not yet seen an Asian before (at least that was the subconscious impression I had)?!

One of the kids clearly read my body language, and he grabbed my arm and showed me this wall on the other side of the boy's dorm. Some kids were handling their private businesses publicly. He too joined the crowd.

Well... I will hold. But at least I found out the answer to John's question earlier. But what if...

Never mind. In hindsight, the "don't ask, don't tell" policy was actually working quite well here!

After all the unexpected hassle, I returned to the stage with a miraculous temporary relief from the stomachache after saying a quick little prayer, and prepared for the worship program. To my surprise, our audiences included not only children but some adults too, mostly female. Don't they have better things to do elsewhere?!

Pastor Mick took out the guitar and played, led, and sang like a pro. Some mosquitoes were interfering but that wasn't too bad. When I was trying to follow his quick change of pace in songs and hand motions like a parrot, a lady spectator was frantically laughing at my retardation.

Hey, thanks for your appreciation! I didn't get through all the troubles to come to Uganda to get mocked at! I gave her a nasty frown, dropping everything that I was supposed to be doing. She caught my frown and stopped laughing.

A few moments after I calmed down, I quietly asked myself: "*Why are you upset at something so trivial? Is your craving for appreciation such a high priority in the middle of a mission trip?*"

There was nothing I could undo. I gathered my composures and thoughts to sing even louder than before, and off-pitch as usual.

The worship program lasted about 45 minutes and as soon as it was over, the majority of the audience stood up and left. It was possibly less appealing or entertaining than they expected.

Truthfully, I didn't even know if they understood any of the things we, or mostly Pastor Mick, said or preached. We did what we were supposed to do, and I could only pray that it did provide some relief, in however entertaining way possible, in their lives.

Soon after a short break, the kids took over the stage and prepared for a much more formal welcome program. The Ugandans were big on orientation and entertaining guests as a way to show hospitality. Our team sat down in some artistic, three-and-a-half-legged chairs in the front row with caution, but there weren't enough chairs.

I felt kind of embarrassed as if I needed to be "welcomed". I stood on the side and was quietly giving high-fives to the kids around me.

A kid in a ripped black t-shirt seemed to be exceptionally thrilled when he noticed my presence. Could I be the first Asian guy he has ever seen? Probably, I mean, I was super aware of my unique appearance and identity since day one. The only "Asian" thing that I spotted from a distance was a restaurant named "Ling Ling" in downtown Kampala when Mr. Chauffer was making the tough turns. And of course, I would never know who was running the eatery.

"Name? Your name?" I tried to ask this kid using hand gestures, first by pointing at myself and said "Am-br-ose", then pointed at him.

He smiled but didn't get it. But he slapped my hands hard for some reason. And boy, was he a strong 5 or 6 years old!

Oh, well, what did it matter. I may never see him again after the end of today anyway, and he may turn his attention to someone else very soon.

"Sacroddnaadnagufosrotisivuoyemoclewew!!! lalalalalala!!!"

The little performers started to get loud and active. I turned around and paid my proper respect.

After a few moments, I saw a man sitting in a chair looking nervous and depressed. I wonder who he was. One of the staff at Dorcas? Or from a nearby church? He was well dressed and looked educated. He saw me looking at his direction but didn't bother to show any facial expression. I took my camcorder out and signaled to him that I was going to take a picture of him. He was looking at me but didn't show much of a response. I went ahead and pressed the shutter button anyway.

I have kept this precious picture in memory and in my photo collections for years, and you shall see why.

Bam pong bam pong bam pong bam pong bam pong... Now a toddler sat on one side of a small self-made drum and hit the sides in an extremely coherent rhythm with his tiny fists.

Impressive.

After 2 more hours of singing in a foreign language, clapping, and dancing from the boys' choir, teenage girls drama team, and a co-ed group, I felt a little dizzy and decided to head back as soon as the ceremonies were all finished. It was still early in the afternoon, and some of the team members chose to stay and hang around. Some wanted to organize a lesson plan or activity for the next several days. My stomachache was coming back, and jet lag has finally rang the doorbell in my system. I surrendered to the natural callings, and took a short nap in my room.

The sky turned dark already when I woke up. It wasn't that late in the evening, but it could get quite depressing and unromantic after the sun hid behind the clouds. I hurried into the dining room, and saw over a dozen people gathered around and engaged in different conversations.

I mingled my way in and found some familiar faces. The doctors who shook my hands passionately from this morning dropped by for dinner along with a few new faces. They were all doctors invited by our hosts, and the newbies were those that just graduated from the Jinja Medical School. Will and Liz threw a party to celebrate their accomplishments.

"I am very proud and grateful of these young men" proclaimed Liz, "they have made a decision to stay in a small town and treat the sick here instead of going to a big city like Mbale to make big money. They know we need doctors and are willing to work long shifts. We couldn't ask for more."

Hats off and humble bow.

On the other end of the room, I eavesdropped a conversation on something totally unrelated: it was about what happened at Dorcas during my nap. I couldn't help to overhear the details: Shirley was obviously devastated over something and Pastor Mick was trying to calm her down.

"You know, my husband and I spent almost 50 bucks on those xeroxed copies, and they were just wasted in less than a minute!" Shirley was venting furiously and looking for some empathy.

"What happened?" I asked Bob, who sat next to me.

"When we were passing out some materials for an arts and crafts lesson this afternoon to the kids, some got really excited and rushed to the front and grabbed them. Everyone else followed and tried to take whatever they could. Everything got ripped apart, and the session basically turned into a mini riot."

"Did anyone get hurt?" I didn't see all 12 of us in the dining room.

"No, praise God, but like Shirley said, the kids torn up everything. We don't even know how we will conduct any lesson plans going forward, if something like this were to happen again. Perhaps we should consult with Liz later."

At least no one got hurt. When Shirley's frantic yelling finally subsided after almost what seemed to be an eternity, I started to ponder on Bob's point. I couldn't make much of a conclusion, and hoped that it was just one exception out of the norm.

Read on, and you'll see.

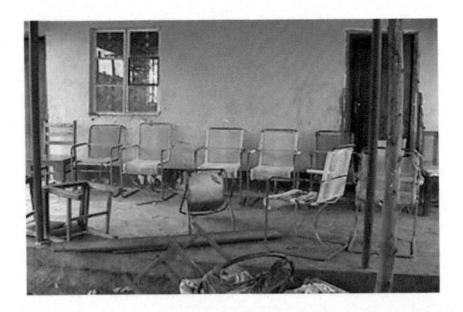

Chapter 05: One Step More

Sunday, April 27th, 2003, @ 8:00am

Usually, by this time on any given Sunday, I would be all washed and dressed up and ready to go to church for its service at 9:15am. That's not happening yet. I was still lying on my bed feeling down and dormant. The little visitors from the corner of the ceiling seemed to have taken off for breakfast hunting. I rolled up my sleeves by half an inch and noted a bite near the end of my left palm. The long sleeves didn't really work, and fortunately my salty blood wasn't all that tasty either to that family of three. Otherwise, there should have been more bites all over my face.

The good part was that I wasn't feeling nauseating, thanks to the prescribed Doxycycline taken ahead of time. From what the British folks told me, one time Mark got bitten during the night and the next morning he was throwing up like mad as soon as he leaped out from bed.

My stomach was doing fine too. No gas, no urges, and it was just as bloated as it had always been. The room was exceptionally quiet. Even Pastor Mick stopped murmuring in his dream or "making music" for a moment. Actually, the whole place was creepily calm.

The random daydreaming was not stopping. *Where is everyone? How about the rooster that always crow regardless of the time of the day?*

Ever since I freaked out after reading the book of 1st Peter, I felt much better for a good old 12 hours. But the time the team spent inside Dorcas depressed me again. Images of the broken chairs, pseudo-bathrooms, malnourished children in torn garment carrying bellies of worms, and the omnipresent mud sticking to everyone's barefoot kept circulating in my head.

And what have I done so far? Getting covered in crap, having cramps, pretending to sing, and being tired most of the time. Wow, that was a lot of achievement.

The problem was, what else could we do for the remainder of the trip? If the program went haywire like how Bob and Shirley described, and if we would need to hold programs or lead activities in an open space like in Dorcas, how much could we improvise and honestly add value to the kids' welfare?

And we haven't really explored the real limitations of the clinic yet. Doctor Doug and Raeanne had for sure, but I had not had a chance to talk to either one of them yet.

Everything was just so out of wrack. God, please grant me the strength to last through today. Just today.

It was more like a plea bargain than a prayer. I had too many questions but too little energy to think through them. Ah, qui sera sera, it's time to get up.

The sun was still hiding behind the clouds, napping.

The surrounding tranquility was something that I had always ignored back home. Why the rush, after all? It was Sunday morning, and I couldn't even practice carpe diem when nobody was around. Was it just me or was it something from the American culture? Or was it both?

I sneaked into the bathroom and took my time to familiarize with the infrastructure inside, a luxury in the absence of competition with my fellow comrades. The entire roll of toilet paper John put next to the potty was soaked, and I was surprised that nothing had chew that thing up yet.

The guesthouse started to get noisy once I finished the daily routine, as if everybody coincidentally woke up, washed up, and dressed up all at the same time. That was good, at least no one had to waste time waiting for anyone for any reason.

During breakfast, our leader has decided to go to a church nearby for worship service at 11 o'clock, per recommendation by Liz. Well, that was good too, most of us had not had the chance to really visit the neighborhood, and we would save time on commute.

Looks like everything was going to run smoothly after a few days of settling in!!!

****

Breakfast was a simple treat of fruit, cereal, and toast with a touch of continental style. We were told that we will come back for lunch and dinner, and there will be a feast waiting. I could care less as long as I wasn't cramping again.

There was still another hour before service, so everyone went back to their rooms during this limbo free time. As I was just loitering around inside the compound, the same well-dressed, depressed guy at Dorcas from yesterday reappeared. A little at awe, our eyes caught each other's attention and I greeted him. For the sake of simplicity, let's call him Conrad.

"Hello, how are you, my American friend?" replied Conrad, without the typical exaggerated enthusiasm from the other local people around. I was flattered by the fact that he acknowledged my identity as an American, even though most of our neighbors still couldn't quite grasp the concept of Asian-Americans.

"I am doing well, thank you. You were at the ceremony yesterday at the children center, right?"

"Yes, I always go there, and I am a student studying at the theological seminary in Kampala," continued Conrad, using an unusually calm but hospitable tone, "I have heard that you and your friends came from America to help us, and you may find this a little unexpected: the next term is starting after summer, but I am not sure if I can continue anymore because I don't have enough sponsorship…"

I looked into his eyes and thought: *"geez, you are pretty straightforward!"*

He probably read the skeptical expression on my face, so he took out and hand over a few pieces of paper. They were documents that showed his record of enrollment from a seminary and some dorm's meal plan card. Of course I wouldn't know how they should look, but they appeared to be official with the letterhead at the top and a dark purple stamped seal on the lower right-hand corner.

"So, how much does it cost for one term?" I wanted to cut to the chase.

"With classes, meals, and room and board, it's about the same as what a minister makes in a month, which is about $40 U.S. dollars." Conrad answered slowly and comprehensively.

Okay, let me think for a second here. He was at Dorcas yesterday and now on Will's and Liz's turf. I had no idea how he got in, but is he their friend? I browsed around and could not find the hosts. Great. Okay, let's assume he was straight up lying; what then? If I decided to give him some support, all he could get from me would be 20 or 40 bucks. This translates to a fancy lunch or dinner in downtown SF (2003 standard). But was he *really* lying?

I studied those documents carefully again and they looked pretty sophisticated. Conrad waited patiently by my side. There were no misspellings, crooked printing, or anything out of the ordinary. What if I refused and he couldn't continue his studies?

The angel on my right shoulder was convincing me to take a chance and give him the benefit of the doubt, if the tradeoff were not unbearable. But common sense, I meant the demon on my other shoulder, was persuading me to pass.

Well, since he had the balls to ask...

"Look Conrad, I don't have a lot of cash with me right now. I can probably sponsor you for a month but not the whole semester. But let me ask my team to see if they can help. Why don't you wait here and I'll see what I can do." I dashed off and try to find the rest of the group for my new venture on this good day, and to see what they may think about this proposal.

Fortunately, most of them were ready to take off for church and stepped out of their rooms. I quickly gathered everyone and announced my project.

Other than Pastor Mick, the rest of the gang seemed adamant about the sponsorship, but still chipped in a little. That was totally fine, since I wasn't entirely certain about this whole deal either. But hey, how could a stranger come in so freely if he weren't at least an acquaintance of the host?

Pastor Mick was the more ecstatic one on the team. I put in $40 and he up the ante to $75!

At the end, more than $200 was collected. That should be good for about six months. I handed the money over to Conrad, and he thanked me and asked for my contact info so he could update me with any news after I returned to the States. It sounded like a feasible idea; if he were really studying, he could inform me about his progress. But if he took the money to smoke pot, it wasn't like he could get a hold of me anyway.

"You two want to take a picture together?" Shirley suggested.

Another excellent idea from someone unexpected.

Conrad, looking as serious as ever, finally poured out a contented look on his face. Perhaps he was a little embarrassed to ask for money from strangers to begin with?

It was indeed a test of faith, regardless of what the outcome will be.

****

The clock soon ticked to 11am and everyone on the team, plus our host, took the "Shared Blessings" van (the organization's "official" vehicle used by the clinic and the children center) and Will's car to head out for worship service. Pastor Mick seemed to be a little more nervous than usual, securing his Bible tightly in his hands.

"Ambrose, can you do me a favor?" Doctor Doug asked when I turned around, "Can you use this camera and take a picture of me when I read the scripture up on the podium during service?"

"Oh, you mean they have asked you to do some serving later?" I had no idea who "they" were though.

"Yeah, and Pastor Mick will be preaching this morning, right after my turn." Doug answered while showing his infectious, confident smile.

"Sure, I guess we'll both have to sit in the first row so I can capture that Kodak moment for you." I took his camera and began to wonder: *was it just me that was always out of the loop because I daydreamed too much, or was there so many last-minute changes going on that internal team communications were never seriously implemented?*

"Brenda, did you know that Pastor Mick is going to preach during service?" I turned around again and randomly found someone that I hadn't spoken with for a long awhile.

"He is? Oh that's good." The calm reply was something I sort of expected.

The short ride ended abruptly as we stepped out of the van literally within minutes after we got in. The church sat between Dorcas and a grade school. We could have walked!

Still very puzzled about some of the arrangements made.

Inside the empty sanctuary stood a couple of ministers and church workers, all in their early 20's, greeted each of us warmly and genuinely.

One of the guys had a weird mix of facial expression; he appeared a little dull but happy. Oh! He had a pair of tilted, oversize glasses on.

My improper stare caught his attention while we were shaking hands, and he was looking at someone else behind me. I turned around, but there was no one there.

"Good morning, how are you doing my brother?" the young minister asked.

"Very well, thank you." After a nanosecond pause, I realized that he was one of the church staff the team met back at Dorcas a couple of days ago. Man, those glasses totally threw me off!

Breaking the awkwardness, the minister was busy showing off his new present: "These glasses have helped me see better. Thanks a lot." He still sounded tired but contented.

"It was part of the donations from us?!" I couldn't hide my enlarged pupils.

But at least he could see much better now, amid his dizziness...

The first 2 rows of bleachers in the sanctuary had been reserved for the American visitors. The worship area in the front was elegantly decorated with bouquets of flowers and the tables were covered with large, white cloths. The cross in the center was made up of two pieces of disproportional red cloth that looked more like a skinny version of the Red Cross logo. The only source of light came from the large windows on the sides, which were large rectangular holes without any glass. The floor was not cemented either, which made the church building feel almost as good as outdoor, had the roof not been built.

The congregation slowly emerged and soon filled the bleachers over and beyond their capacity. Some kids were sitting directly in front of the stage next to the choir, and those that couldn't get in were watching from outside through the open windows. The facility was overcrowded, but was unusually quiet. It was nothing like the chit-chat noises and socializing you can always hear before service starts back home.

Next came the best part: a service in the local dialect that got me into playing another guessing game! Well, it wasn't all that bad. In fact, the choir members soon took over after some introduction and put on a Broadway show! A teenager played a big drum, and each of the choir members was clapping, waving, singing, and even dancing as if they were performing during the Superbowl half time show. God, that energy was amazing!

The locals told me after the service that they performed like this not because there are guests visiting. It happens on a regular basis.

Doctor Doug's and Pastor Mick's turn didn't come until after about half an hour later when the choir finally got exhausted from showing off their praises. Carefully fulfilling my promise to Doctor Doug, I sat back and listened to Pastor Mick's sermon. It was all figurative and I must confess that it was a mediocre delivery. When the interpreter was translating each sentence to what it sounded like a million words in a second, my attention diverted from the small commotion on the side. No, the noises did not come from the Americans, but kids that pushed their faces against the fences on the windows. I turned my head to the other side and realized that the sanctuary was even more packed than I last looked. The kids by the windows didn't seem to want to give up their spots no matter what, and I timidly shook and lowered my head.

The contrasts were simply too overwhelming. From the eagerness to worship on everyone's face to the determination of the choir members, the shame that casted a shadow on my head was making me look the other way. *Why have I been going to church for in the last 2 decades? It was more like a ritual.* If I could just convince you to come over here and show you- that would be more persuasive than a thousand words.

The service ended by 1pm and the "Shared Blessings" van was nowhere to be found nearby. I could care less and wanted to hang around like everybody else on the grass outside the church building, to add a few collections to the team's photo album. The folks around me were speaking extremely loudly- now that was something universal.

Being the only "exotic" Asian guy (no, it's not like what you can find online) standing around with a camcorder in my hand caught the attention of several friendly teenagers. To my surprise, none wanted to check out my camcorder, and some only wanted to say "ha-llo". Like Halifa, that was probably as far as the exchange could get. As more and more kids gathered around me, I asked Bob to take a picture even though I felt somewhat odd. Kids here would never refuse to take a picture with a foreign stranger, which made me wondered. Thanks to digital camcorders, they could at least see the replay immediately on the screen, and be amazed and overjoyed momentarily.

The van finally showed up and took us back to the guesthouse. About half way through, Arlene asked some of us to get off because the van needed to pick something up from a nearby store. The younger folks, including myself, started to walk along with dozens of other local people on the muddy road in front of Dorcas.

A cheerful boy suddenly sneaked to my left-hand side and tagged along. Oh, it was the same boy from yesterday morning at the children center. I recognized the same torn black, white, and green stripes T-shirt with the solid black short sleeves. His smile was super innocent, but the pointy teeth were really messed up.

"Hi! What-is-your-name?" In a very slow tempo, I couldn't resist to try my luck.

"???"

Of course.

Just when I was about to give up, a young man gave me a hand and decoded my question to Alan- yup, that was his name.

"How old are you?" I was getting greedy, but the volunteer didn't mind.

This time, Alan extended his arm and opened his hand to show me all his fingers and palm. He should be in kindergarten, like how I guessed.

The short exchange ended abruptly when Alan continued to walk straight and I made a left turn. Not sure if I will ever see him again. I smiled and waved anyway, and Alan was still as cheerful as before.

Everyone on the team dragged their famished stomachs into the dining room, and trays of   traditional Ugandan dishes like matoke and broiled tilapia were all ready to be served. There was this other rice dish with chunks of meat and bone that nobody was able to tell what it was, until Will revealed the truth.

"It's fried rice with goat and avocado. It was from one of the goats in our backyard." Will announced the final answer with a sense of pride.

"Cool!" If Will told us it was a jaguar or a wild lion from a nearby marketplace, my face would have immediately turned blue.

The ladies were apparently not as enthusiastic as Will. They were starved like everyone else, but made their moves slowly to the buffet table. Some went to the side table and grabbed some drinks instead.

The diced avocado was a blast when mixed with the somewhat gamey, dehydrated goat pieces. The rice and the meaty juice wrapped around these chunks of extravaganza added a touch of the soggy flavor that took my taste buds to a whole new level of excitement. Will, damn it, you're the man!

Goat / lamb / mutton had to be the king of meats. Its distinctive taste and fragrance are not comparable to any other common choices available in the restaurants, regardless if it's the rack, shoulder, leg, or stew. Beef has its unique flavors too, but the zest is just not as addicting to lamb. Chicken and pork were more or less interchangeable.

I took advantage of the monopoly when my potential competitors retreated without even attempting to start any battles.

A full stomach certainly made me happier after the pooping problem vanished.

It was a short, necessary mental and physical break.

****

"What? Another welcome ceremony?" I woke up from my food coma and was dazed after hearing that soon there will be another one of those never-ending occasions.

"We'll be doing some worshipping and giving some of the candies away too." Someone added.

"You think it'll be okay?" Recalling from the mini-riot less than 24 hours ago, someone else asked an intelligent question.

"We'll just have to hand them out more carefully. The Jolly Rancher was starting to melt."

The latter suggestion sounded sensible, although I had no idea how "careful" we can be. *Should we bring a knife or something?* The red devil on my left shoulder probed my obscure curiosity to find out first-hand how bad things could turn out to be, so I questioned no further.

The team returned to the broken chairs on the stage inside Dorcas, and I quickly claimed a seat since my legs likely would not be able to hold my fat torso for more than an hour. Once I figured out how to balance myself on the shaky chair, I looked up to the surrounding environment and felt the panic attack again.

It's the same old story: everything remained to look run down, the malnourished kids with unlimited energy in torn clothes, the unfathomable cruelty and irony that were lying blatantly in front of my eyes, and I failed to put forth any action other than being sarcastic or judgmental. *God, what should I do now?*

Relax, Ambrose. Enjoy the show. It will be good. The little voices in my head instructed me to calm down with these short commands.

A co-ed group of about a dozen gathered in front of us and started singing. This time, reportedly, a quick song in English to start with. *Whatever*, I thought to myself, with my head down, *"it's all the same to me…"*

♫*"One step more, one step more,
Give me faith for one step more,
One step more my Savior one step more,
Faith for one step more."*♫

"What?!"

An electric current zapped through my whole body. I turned my head up in no time and looked at the singers in disbelief. They were singing the second chorus already, but I couldn't pay attention to the lyrics anymore. The words that I just heard were circulating inside my head non-stop. My internal temperature continued to rise and I started to sweat. The accelerated breathing pattern alarmed me to calm down and respond to the epiphany.

How dumbfounded I was! I ignored the core of my conviction! Who cares if there will be a riot? Who cares if I will get sick again in the middle of no man's land? So what if all of our plans went astray and we were stuck in limbo? What has Jesus taught me for the last several years?

The graceful slap on the face from God and the kids was unexpectedly fast and effective.

The best part of this episode was that I wasn't the only one that felt the grace of God. My female teammates were especially touched by the powerful lines and the simple melody. Doctor Doug was so impressed that he later took out his own precious, backup camcorder and asked the kids to repeat the song. And all this time I thought he was an amateur with that little machine like how he told everyone else!

If there were a need for reconciliation among any team members, that could not have been a better time. That was my gut feeling.

****

The first thing I needed to do was to smile more frequently. It felt like such a long time ago already, and my cheek muscle was a little stiff. It was so foolish of me to have let that happen.

After the children finished performing, it was the team's turn. It was kind of like the first worship, except there wasn't a rehearsal. Since Pastor Mick was going to repeat the same procedures, it went by smoothly and hassle-free.

After about half an hour or so, Pastor Mick stopped playing the guitar and muttered a few words with Arlene on the side.

Yup, it looked like it was about time to distribute the candies. But how?

To my BIG surprise, it wasn't any rocket science. We each took a bag of the hard and sticky Jolly Rancher candy and gave out *one* piece at a time to each individual sitting down.

Guess what happened within a few seconds after we started doing that?

When the crowd at the back realized what was going on, all of them sprinted to the front and tried to grab a piece of whatever they could get. I doubted if they could see that those were only candies, but that didn't deter them. They knew *something* was being handed out, and only a fool would ignore a freebie.

Dozens of them surrounded each of the Santa Claus, including myself, and the crowd got bigger and attracted even more people to try to get whatever they could. Looking back, the situation was exactly how Shirley described. The only difference was that our audience didn't rip the candies nor the Santa Claus apart.

I had no time to find out how the other team members were handling the situation. For the first few moments my sub-consciousness was still prompting me to figure out a way to deliver the candies fairly. The younger toddlers were pushed to the ground but planted themselves sturdily on their knees, forgetting the pushing and other offenses their older peers have done and begged to receive that unknown sweet that would last less than five minutes in their months.

The older ones, including teenagers that were strong enough to beat the crap out of anyone, were surrounding me on their feet firmly and tried to bargain for one extra piece with no convincing argument. I took my right hand out from the bag and grab it tightly with my left hand, in a desperate attempt to escape from the scary chaotic scene. During the whole fiasco, I was anticipating that someone would either punch me in the face or just rob that gift bag, but that never happened. For a split second I thought about throwing the bag up into the air and let the kids pick up whatever they could off the ground.

No, no, no, that would be very screwed up. These were the kind of crazy ideas that would pop up with when someone was in the same helpless dilemma.

Pastor Mick picked up his guitar and started playing after realizing that the plan was not working out. All the Santa Claus hurried back onto the stage and pretended nothing had happened. The crowd soon realized they weren't going to get any freebies, so some of them also returned to their seats, while some disappeared without a trace. After another song or so, the team wrapped up and went back to the guesthouse, disappointed and speechless.

I wondered if the local realized how the lose-lose situation evolved. I also wondered what the team has learnt from these lessons. As for myself, I just felt particularly sad for the preschoolers. All this hassle for a piece of candy? What kind of a world are we living in?

The team gathered in the dining room, tried to evaluate what happened, and to figure out what should be done next. Nobody commented on the stupidity (or the "pitfalls") of the arrangement. We still had a huge bag of the melting Jolly Rancher, along with other teaching materials that were supposedly to be handed out for the classroom activities from the pre-planned lessons.

One of the ladies told me: "You know what, Ambrose, you should have gone outside to the grass area when you were passing out the candies."

"One step more, one step more, give me faith for one step more…" I could only recite these lines silently before I exploded.

Fortunately, before I could react, one of the other ladies responded: "Well, that would not have made a difference, wouldn't it?"

Thank you Lord.

No one seemed to really have a viable answer on how to properly allocate the crayons, papers, little toys, and the remaining supplies going forward. At the end, Arlene decided to leave all of them to Liz, whom seem to be the best candidate to determine who, when, and how to share the supplies effectively.

Fair enough. But how should we carry out the lesson plans without the nuts and bolts? I couldn't ask this question. I didn't have the slightest hint to put forth a suggestion.

Dinner was a little bit more conservative than lunch, with some common dishes like spinach, rice, and fried chicken, in addition to salads and matoke. Shirley was apparently more relieved, when she finally voiced out her thoughts: "The lamb for lunch was okay, but it was a bit gamey."

"Have some chicken then", I murmured to myself. On the brighter side, at least we didn't get to hear her complaining about the riots anymore.

"You know what, Ambrose, there is something that we need to tell you." Arlene and a few other ladies, sitting in a half circle, suddenly asked for my participation in their conversation.

"Yes?"

"Conrad, the guy from this morning, was a conman."

"***What?!***"

"He's a fake. He always comes to this area to do this kind of cheating and swindling."

"How come he could just come in and out of Dorcas and the guesthouse so freely and nobody said anything about him?" Something wasn't making sense to me here.

"It's not like back home in the U.S. Anyone can basically go in and out here." The "no-duh!" expression on whoever chipped in to Arlene's amazing induction surely wasn't satisfying. I just felt bad for those who contributed to the scam, especially Pastor Mick.

There was no way to decipher the local protocols. For the next week or so, just try whatever.

Arlene came by to console me while I was sitting down and trying to think the whole ordeal over. "I am alright," my shaky voice probably didn't really persuade her, "remembering a short story written by Leo Tolstoy, I am glad that I didn't go as far as what the main character did." I tried to sound sophisticated.

Arlene became interested: "What is it about?"

"I can't remember the title of the story, but it was a short piece about this devil trainee in an attempt to screw up a devout farmer living a simple life. One day, he stole the farmer's lunch while he was working in the field, hoping to hear that he would curse God for his misfortune. But when the farmer found out his lunch was missing, he only said that he hopes whoever was hungry enough to have taken his lunch will be blessed. This little devil was reprimanded by Master Satan, but was given another chance to make sure that the farmer would become a hater in 3 years. So the rookie disguised himself as a diligent young man to work for the farmer, and because of his advices the farmer has become a rich man in merely 3 years. To celebrate his own success, the farmer threw a party and invited everyone in town, and he became arrogant, egotistic, and offensive to the point where everyone just left him. Satan was overjoyed to see this transformation and asked what the little devil has done. "Nothing," he replied;" these attributes are all embedded in the human nature, and my job was to bring them out into the open."."

My eloquence to verbally recite an old story was probably horrible beyond imagination, and Arlene appeared to have understood only half of what I just told her. It didn't matter, so I concluded: "let's just hope that I wouldn't become the farmer that subsequently turned into a hater."

Still, it hurts when you find out the awful truth after you have taken a proactive step to be generous.

I headed straight to bed after the conversation to beat Pastor Mick to sleep, so that his snoring wouldn't get in the way. Neither did I want to tell him the truth about Conrad (he did eventually find out and reacted "normally"). I wrapped myself completely inside the blanket to guard against the little insects on the ceiling, and noticed that my fingernails were all covered in black. Crap, did I touch something dirty? I was totally drained from the eventful day and couldn't recall. I looked up to the mosquito family, stuck out and waved a finger, and whispered: "If you guys want to suck my blood tonight, make sure you start from the tip of my middle finger!"

How idiotic.

So much for the tranquil day that started at 8am this morning.

Ambrose Tse

Chapter 06: The Real Deal

One thing I forgot to emphasize more scrupulously thus far was the daily rain it had been regularly pouring either during the afternoon or early evening. The rainy season had proved faithful even to the most precise point in time, making sizzling Africa consistently cool during our stay. With the unexpected comfort Mother Nature brought upon, it was easy to forget some of the daily routines one must perform regardless where s/he is. An example of that would be taking a short, rejuvenating shower.

That was how my dirty fingernails evolved, after 5 days of letting the gentle breeze conveniently dry my perspiration. Much like a skunk, I couldn't smell my own odor either. And I didn't realize the need to shower until I noticed the dark, smudgy stuff accumulated in my finger nails were exactly the same substance that was collected when I scratched the back of my itchy neck.

No wonder there were no communications between me and the rest of the team.

The main problem was not so much about the hassle of sharing a bathroom with four other dudes. It had more to do with developing a viable plan to use the facility.

The other thing I forgot to mention was the way these deluxe guest bathrooms were built. There was a potty (or a toilet in the rooms where the ladies stayed in), a sink, and a showerhead attached to the wall, but there was no designated area for showering. Meaning that once you start to shower, you would need to "kick" the water into the potty every once awhile to prevent the bathroom from over-flooding. And with the water splashes, who knows what little animals might be evacuating from their hideout inside the potty and say hello.

Plus, even though I brought a brand new pair of water shoes designed for situations like this, it still felt awkward. No, "awkward" wasn't the right adjective. The word "kinky" was a better description. Under what circumstances would anyone be completely naked and wear shoes? I meant, I have *absolutely never* seen anyone in that kind of outfit, under most circumstances. Even back in college days, people didn't shower with sandals on in the dorm bathroom. Avoiding that kinky feeling outweighed the need to keep good hygiene habits.

And what about getting the whole bathroom floor wet? Who was going to clean up? With what? My tongue? How long would it take? Who could I ask for help?

The growing and tantalizing itch was telling me to just find a quiet time today to take a shower first, and figure the out the methodology later.

****

The third item that I forgot to mention was the general norm that people usually do not watch TV during a short-term mission trip. I never bothered to ask why, and I have not heard anyone requested the hosts even to watch the news. Will probably had a TV in his room, but the team and I tended to go to sleep unusually early, like 10pm or 11pm, at the very latest because of rotational blackout every night. Result? Group morning devotion scheduled to take place at 7:30am before breakfast.

That actually wasn't so bad. With more than 8 hours of sleep each night, I was quite well rested and ready to go the very next day. The main problem again was: where could we go?

Well, the show must go on, and we will start with Brenda for this morning's session. Brenda was a special ed teacher, and could teach with zeal and little help from anyone or with anything. Being the camcorder man / photographer, I will have to tag along.

86

As things quickly normalized on a Monday, Arlene told the team that there should be just the regular attendees at Dorcas, which totaled about less than 50 in the morning. They had some sort of morning routines to deal with, so we couldn't intrude until about 11am.

We, including Brenda, Denise, and Allison, left the guesthouse at about 10:30am and made our way out. It was another comfortable, peaceful day to start with. It was so relaxing that the crap from the last few days seemed to have already vanished from memory.

Oops! The classroom wasn't quite ready yet, and we thought we could get ourselves prepared by showing up about 15 minutes earlier. We'll just play with the kids a bit if they have the time.

The kids did have the time. A snack break is scheduled once in the late morning and once in the late afternoon during the weekdays. And by "snacks" it had always been a cup of brown, thick, and murky liquid that looked like hot cocoa. The timing for snack breaks couldn't have been smarter, if you think about it.

"Gimme five!" I extended my right arm to a little boy that had been starring at me for some time. He stopped drinking and continued to stare.

Okay, let's try this again. This time, I also extended my left arm and twisted my palm to slap onto my other palm, where I essentially clapped my hands and hoped that he would get my hint.

He didn't, but the boy next to him did. And he smacked my hand as hard as he could to leave me a good impression. Considered the energy exerted, my wrist would have been broken if he were a few years older.

I immediately retrieved the skills learned from my drama class back in high school and put on an exaggerated face of being injured. My eyes wide shut and half of my tongue hanging out, with my wrist shaking violently from left to right. The madman look was something I missed doing for the longest time.

Both of them laughed frantically.

The first kid copied his predecessor and I repeated what I did, and they laughed even harder. Boy, didn't they love to see people getting tortured.

Things were getting dried after the third round, so when they swung their punches I stepped back to make them missed. Then I pointed with both index fingers and pretended to laugh at them. In their astonishment, they turned into serious little featherweight boxers and tried harder.

"Ouch!" It started to become dangerously painful, and the noises we made were attracting way too much attention from the small wishful and curious eyes around. The double team did not appear to give up until they see some blood or bruises, so the best alternative was to stop and move on.

I gave them a gentle pad on their backs as I unilaterally decided to end the semi-sadistic game. Their eyes were questioning my verdict, but didn't insist on continuing the fun.

It was a good old 2 minutes, regardless.

The boy's dorm was right ahead as I slowly walked away from the crowd. It was a small cabin separately built to the side of the main classroom. A group of about 15 boys from different and unknown backgrounds called this "home". No one from the team was invited to go inside the last time we visited. Should I go in and take a peek?

Ha! The ladies had already gathered themselves there, along with one of the teachers on duty, giving them the details about the dorm, the boys, etc.

I squeezed myself through the ladies after greeting them and got to the door, but soon realized that there was no way that anyone could go inside.

A rusty bike was parked at the front, leaving less than a foot of space for a chubby guy like me to get through between the bike and a bed. Area of the room was roughly 80 square feet, and 4 beds, 2 of which were bunk bed sets, were tightly fit around the parameter, leaving enough empty space to perhaps fit half a bed in the middle. The law of entropy reigned over the boys' bedroom, and there were no dressers or shelves to put things into.

Wait a minute now- those weren't bunk beds! A bed was stacked on top of the other to make it look like bunk beds. The mattresses the boys were sleeping on weren't mattresses either. They looked like some kind of old, yellowish foam that are normally used as packaging materials inside a big TV box or something. Okay, so the boys were sleeping on these pseudo-mattresses in a cramped room with stuff lying and hanging all over the place.

As usual the floor wasn't paved neither. It was flattened maybe by some sort of flooring materials, but you can still smell the mud and see the dirt quite easily.

Same old story. I was gradually transforming into a stoic.

The tour ended when the time for class has finally come. Brenda, Denise, and Allison seemed to know exactly what to do, so the only help I could offer was to take some pictures from the outside of the excessively overcrowded classroom. Even though I had no idea what program they had in mind, it should be exciting. Finally! Isn't this what all of us came here for?!

Brenda and Allison quickly gathered all 30-or-so students to sit on the floor of this classroom that was slightly smaller than the boy's dorm we just visited. For those that couldn't or didn't want to go in, Denise was watching after them out in the open.

I took my camera out and was prepared to take some candid shots.

Wait, where's the translator?! Do we have one? If not, how the heck can we get this thing going?!

Brenda snapped away my anxiety instantly by extending both of her arms in mid-air and succinctly delivered a Bible story in a strong and dramatic voice. The class listened attentively and quietly. One of the local teachers sneaked in and helped with the translations. I took a deep breath and sighed in relief.

There wasn't much physical movement going on with Brenda's bible story-telling, and it looked like the lesson would continue in this format for the next half hour. I took a couple of pictures and retreated to where Denise was sitting with a few young girls, which was only a few feet outside of the classroom.

"Where did Allison go?" I asked Denise.

"She went somewhere to look after other kids." Denise replied softly, holding a sleepy infant in her arms.

I kept quiet and chose a semi-unbroken chair to sit next to them. As soon as my butt touched the seat, I jumped back up right away and realized what needed to be done.

It was the buzzing noise enveloping the surrounding from our little friends in search for food in the air. There were dozens of them, literally, from flies, mosquitoes, and other unknown insects.

They were starting to piss me off.

Thanks to Bob's advice during one of those meetings in Modesto, I went to a sporting goods store and bought a mosquito spray with 100% deeds, versus the commonly available ones that had only a weak 5% to 20%. This solid stuff claimed to be extremely effective against mosquitoes. In addition to the Doxycycline, I put a little bit on every single day. But it stunk pretty badly, so I only used them once in the morning.

I stepped into the heavily concentrated "buzzing" zone outside of the classroom door and started swinging my arms in a circle like a madman, in the faintest hope that these insects would disperse and never return. Or, more accurately speaking, at least not in the vicinity where all these kids were.

Futile efforts, of course. Why would these guys go away from their main food sources just because I put on a scary face and swung my arms?

Denise was watching at a distance, amused by my irrational behavior. She didn't say anything, but the corner of her lips moved sixteenth of an inch upward (yes, exactly 1/16). After about 30 seconds, I gave up and returned to the broken furniture, breathless.

What a fool I was.

Gasping for air from the violent activity I put myself through, my attention returned to the few kids chilling in the open. Suddenly, mini-Beyonce emerged from nowhere and clung her back against a column. Then, she wrapped her arms around the column and started shaking her lower torso and legs as if she was trying out some moves. She kept doing that for several minutes and won't stop! Damn, I bet you if she caught the attention of some talent agency in the U.S., she could kick anyone's butt easy.

I put my attention back to the classroom to check out how the lesson plan progressed after realizing the unwarranted digression. I haven't heard any screams from Brenda yet, so

91

everything should be moving along just fine. What was going on though? It was too quiet to be true.

The students were listening attentively to both Brenda and the interpreter. She was acting out the story of Noah and his Ark with a piece of pink cloth on her head. All by herself? Damn, she could have asked some of us to help out. A few minutes later, she passed out some paper and crayons and asked the kids to draw some pictures.

Brenda probably didn't see me peaking through the windows, but it felt kind of creepy to intrude like that for too long. I turned my head away and saw another familiar face. You guessed it- it was Alan, wearing the same ripped T-shirt with the black, green, and white stripes.

"Hello Alan!" I exploited the vibe that has been slowly forming inside my body.

"Malambe." Alan responded softly, with the cutest smile on his face.

"Gimme five!" I was leveraging on my old trick, extending my hand out at the same time. But Alan didn't quite get it. Instead, he climbed onto the chairs and the table and just moving around without any apparent reason. Could "malambe" mean something other than hello?

I didn't give up. I approached Alan and shook his hand. Then, I did my mischievous thing and tickled his palm with my index finger.

"Argh!" Alan frantically screamed as he hurriedly retracted his arm with a happy but confused look on his face. Someone could probably hear him from 2 miles away.

This had to be the best day of my trip.

"Shhh!" I opened my eyes wide open and put a finger on my lips, while extending my arm again. Boy, this could go on for hours.

Alan, like many other kids I later encountered, didn't suspect my motive until about the third time. He was having way too much fun, and I stopped before Brenda came out to smack me, figuratively.

"Malambe!" I waved right in front of Alan's eyes, hoping to figure out what the word meant.

"Malambe*." Alan again responded softly. I need to ask Will what the word means later.

I took out my camcorder and asked Denise to take a picture of me and Alan. I then showed him the replay on the screen and he was just as happy as ever. To him, I am THE most exotic Asian that he has never ever seen before.

Commotions from the classroom started to grow, and I gave Alan a little hug and waved goodbye. I couldn't tell if he understood what it meant. All I could say was that I won't feel bad if I don't ever see him again.

I rushed back to the classroom and saw that each of the kids was holding a crayon and a piece drawing of some sort in his / her hands. *Phew!* I went in and asked how I could help to clean up, and Brenda asked me to collect the crayons back from each student.

One by one, the little hands surrendered their little utensils and put them into a plastic box. I wondered what they could draw with just one crayon. After I turned around and started to sort them out, suddenly someone grabbed and pulled my camera bag.

Oh crap, don't tell me it was going to be like the riot that took place a day ago!

Within split seconds, I reflexively put my hand onto the camera bag and turned to my right. It was a little girl notifying me that I forgot to collect the crayon she was using.

"Oh, thank you." I nodded and tried to smile, but my neck was hurting a bit.

That girl smiled back and walked away.

"You just gave them each a crayon to draw something?" I asked Brenda while she was still collecting the drawings.

"It was an outline of the Noah's Ark. They just need to fill it in with colors."

"But they each only had one crayon?" I was truly baffled.

"They were trading the crayons with each other. See-" Brenda randomly picked a few and showed some of the colorful artwork. I have never imagined that the Noah's Ark could be purple and orange.

"Aren't they creative?"

"Sure they are. How was class?"

"Very well. Most of them were very quiet. The best part was that it was in order. Even though there wasn't really enough space or crayons for everyone, they learnt to share. When a boy tried to keep a crayon for himself, others told on him!"

'That's good." It all sounded like a brand new concept to me. When was the last time I had to share my stationery with anyone? It was so out of the ordinary.

"Already, I think we are done here. Let's head back." commented Brenda.

****

When we return to the guesthouse, most of the team had come back either from the clinic or somewhere else, and finished lunch. It was all good. I was contented enough that my stomach hasn't acted up at all lately.

Here comes Raeanne the nurse- oh, I almost forgot to ask her for something.

"Hi Raeanne. How was your day so far?"

"Not bad; but I am not quite done yet. I still have to go back to the clinic."

"I see. I was just wondering if you could do me a small favor?" I lowered my voice.

"Yes?" My tone ignited some curiosity in Raeanne's eyes.

"You know that all 5 of us guys were sharing a bathroom with a semi-broken lock, right? Is it okay for me to take a shower in your bathroom this afternoon while you are gone?" I could hardly hear my own voice.

"Sure! No problem, and I don't think my roommate has come back yet. And if she does while you are showering, just put a note on the door beforehand." Raeanne gave me a loud and clear answer.

"Great. Thanks." I ran off to get my clean clothes at once.

I should have asked Raeanne how things work in the bathroom before I let her go, but I was too shy and forgot. There was no shower area per se as expected, only a shower head and a hole on the floor for drainage. What the heck am I suppose to do? Take a 15-minute shower and spend another hour cleaning up the bathroom afterwards? The sun didn't come out today, so even if I left the windows open it will take forever for the place to dry.

Dear reader: for the sake of brevity, I will skip the details of my shower experience. Please do not try to visualize the way I cleaned myself if you do not want to puke.

I managed to get out after 45 minutes, leaving myself somewhat in sweat and the bathroom semi-moist. It felt so much better than before anyhow.

Dinner was supposed to be ready in a couple of hours, but everyone pretty much finished what they were supposed to do and already came back for the day by 5pm. It was one of those hours in the day that depresses people the most. It was getting dark outside but not totally pitch black yet. If you were working in the office, you could either be on your way home or enjoying happy hour in a bar with friends or colleagues. If not, you would be either cooking dinner or watching TV while waiting for dinner to be served. Either way, your blood sugar level would most likely be at the lowest around sunset time.

Piles of arts and crafts ingredients were stacked up against a wall in the dining room, and there won't be any viable channels to pass them out for art projects. Bob and some ladies decided to make the end products and let Liz distribute them to whoever she believed appropriate. Someone brought bags of beads and balls of strings, so the logical thing to do was to make bracelets out of them.

"What are you guys doing?" I asked Bob while wiping off the sweat after the shower.

"Come join us; we've hundreds of bracelets to make out of these beads."

"Okay... I have never made stuff like this before, can you show me how?"

"Here- take a look at this," replied Brenda, "first, get one of each of these colored beads," I glanced over and noted a red, a white, a black, a green, and a yellow bead; "you see the little hole in the middle of each of these beads? Put them through like the ones we have already finished- in that order, and tie a knot at the end. It's really simple."

"Hmmm...okay, let me give it a shot." I was still trying to find out the right way to tie the miniature knot.

I paused after awhile when my counterparts' performance clearly indicated that my skill was no match to theirs. The dexterity required to make these stuff fast and clean were results of years of practice in sewing and doing chores around the house. It just wasn't for me.

What's worse was my shivering fat fingers and deteriorating dry eyes. Whenever I try to pierce the string through the beads, it often took 3 or 4 times. But the *worst* of all was tying the knot at the end. Some of the knots I tied were as big as the size of the combined beads! Consequently, I made bracelets, rings, and necklaces of all sizes for children from age 3 to 13.

"Are these for giants or what?" Bob, unexpectedly serious, demanded an answer while pointing at several irregular sized "bracelets" I just made.

Suddenly, I felt like ignoring him.

After a few moments of awkward silence, one of the ladies broke the ice: "Oh, we can give some of these to the younger children, and they can put them around their necks or something."

"Oh, really?!" I asked myself sarcastically. I remained quiet for another 10 minutes, and told everyone that I got other stuff to take care of. Fortunately, the acting skills I learned from corporate America helped me to leave the table rather diplomatically, but the fume trapped inside my head needed a place to vent.

Geez, thanks for wrapping up my almost perfect day with a blow like this. Unlike the past few days, I was getting pissed off more often instead of feeling sad or helpless.

After a swift dinner, I sat on the bed and contemplated on what needed to be done to end the day without the unresolved emotion lingering around. Apparently, I forgot to go back to the basics. I crawled to the end of the bed and reached for the carry-on bag that has the Bible in it. Which book or scripture should I turn to? I kept flipping through the pages and hoped that a **bolded** title like "**conflict resolution**" would catch my attention. That didn't happen until I almost got to the end, when I finally noticed a topic in the book of Romans. It's called "**Love**".

Love. How corny. But how appropriate.

I started reading from Chapter 12, verse 9: *"Love must be sincere. Hate what is evil; cling to what is good. Be devoted to one another in brotherly love. Honor one another above yourselves. Never be lacking in zeal, but keep your spiritual fervor, serving the Lord. Be joyful in hope, patient in affliction, faithful in prayer. Share with people who are in need. Practice hospitality."*

I hoped I am not going to ever forget about this.

*Malambe means "Peace be with you."

Chapter 07: Dead Day

Crap.

My throat was soring. I knew it! It must have been the wind- not those produced by Pastor Mick, but rather from the open windows while I was showering. I caught a cold.

How bad was it? Just a little dizzy and exhausted, in addition to a dry mouth. My legs didn't feel like moving either, but my body temperature and stomach felt normal.

"Ah…guess what guys?" I was hoping that either Pastor Mick or Bob was awake and could hear me moan.

"What?" Both voices responded, almost simultaneously.

"What time is it now?"

"It just passed six."

"Wow, so early. Oh, I was going to say that I am not feeling too well and probably have to skip breakfast. But I should be okay after awhile."

"Are you having another stomachache?" Bob asked.

"No, it's more like a cold. I was feeling the chill a little bit after showering yesterday."

"You need some Tylenol?"

"Sure do. But let me see how I feel after sleeping in a bit longer."

"Let me know if you'll need anything else."

"I will. Thanks."

I took a deep breath and prayed that the soreness was only an illusion, that I was actually thirsty, and my leg muscles would be reenergized after some more rest. I couldn't imagine how anyone could recuperate from a cold, assuming it was really a simple cold and nothing else, in the middle of a jungle. Sure, Doctor Doug could give me some over the counter medicine and instruct me to let my metabolism naturally fight off the bacteria, but the thought of not having access to the usual, typical resources was horrifying enough to deal with.

There was nothing else I could do but to pray for a speedy recovery.

Half an hour later, nothing seems to have improved, but I did get a mental boost.

"Your folks are on the phone right now." Bob handed over the headset after leaving the bedroom shortly. I climbed down and went out the door to find an open space for the call. I bite the bullet and decided not to let anyone in my family know about my conditions.

"Hello?" I yelled as hard as I could, after hearing some random static passing through from the other end of the headset.

(The original conversation was carried out in my mother tongue language, so the following translation was only an approximation.)

"Son? Is that you?"

"Yes mom. Good morning. What time is it at your place?"

"It's passed 10 o'clock at night. I haven't heard from you for almost a week. You didn't call and I worry about you. Is everything alright?"

"I am doing fine here. It's kind of tough to find a phone here, so I couldn't call. Everything is just different here, you know." What a way to start the morning as a sick liar.

"How was the food? Was your stomach acting up?"

"It's doing alright. In fact, there wasn't much food available, so I ended up eating less and lost some weigh. Ha ha."

"That's good. How's the weather? I couldn't find out any current news about Uganda."

"It's fine. It's now the rainy season, so the temperature is usually about 28 degree Celsius." This was my first sentence in the dialogue with nothing but the truth.

"Did you see any kids?"

"Plenty. There are probably over a few hundred. We had trouble managing some lesson plans though. But we are making progress."

"Okay, remember to take care of yourself and don't take any risk. Call us before you come back when you get a chance, okay?"

"I will. Most likely when we have a layover in London. Who else is there?"

"Dad and sis. Would you like to talk to them?"

"Please."

"Hang on."

"Hello?"

103

"Dad? How's everyone back home?"

"We are doing fine. How's Uganda?"

"Very different than what I perceived. But the people and the country are lovely as expected."

"Hmm... okay, just take good care of yourself, okay? I'll see you at the airport when I pick you up, okay?" Being a college lecturer, dad's schedule had always been flexible during the weekdays.

"You are planning to pick me up? Okay, thanks!"

"You want to speak with sis?"

"Sure."

"Hang on."

Conversation with dad has always been brief.

"What's up?"

"Not much, just tired. It's not even 7am in the morning yet here. Did you just hear a rooster crow?" Roosters in Uganda crow pretty much whenever they please.

"Yeah, it was loud. I am sure mom already asked all the questions for everyone. Anything to add?"

"Yeah, honestly, the condition here is pretty bad, with all the poor kids suffering and dying for no reason and no one gives a crap about them. This place is just like hell." My voice was trembling.

"...well, that's why you guys are there." The former college peer counselor pointed to the right direction.

"True, but resources are extremely limited. We'll do our best. I will touch base more with you when I come back. It's only one more week left."

"Okay, take care now."

"Sure, and thanks for calling. Tell mom not to worry. I will be fine."

"Sure. Bye now."

"Bye."

How I wished the call was longer, even if I had to repeat myself thrice, and I was dying to take a massive dump.

"You caught up with your folks?" Bob came out from the bedroom and asked, after the loud conversation in a foreign language ended.

"Yup..." I sighed in disappointment after hanging up. Probably won't get to talk to them again until I get back to the States.

"Hey Bob, you have something quick and easy for a growling stomach? My stomach is really acting up but I don't want to take away Doctor Doug's time for his patients. You have anything handy?" I pressed my hand against the stomach to show and tell.

"Okay..." I followed Bob back to the bedroom, where he took out a few packs of Pepto Bismo and asked me to chew on a couple. Those pink, powdery tablets- I have never learned to trust that stuff, but there was no other choice available.

I swallowed a few and asked Bob to let everyone know that I will skip breakfast and take a day off. It was also a day for some serious spiritual reorganization.

I hopped right back to bed and tried to knock myself out. My mind was still filled with all kinds of thoughts that I couldn't break loose. After an hour of tossing and turning on bed, one of the young doctors from the clinic knocked on the door and asked to see how I was doing.

Oh great, I saved Doctor Doug's time but wasted the other's. Luckily, the doctor assured me that it wasn't so busy over at the clinic, or else he would not have come.

I slowly sat up and reported the generic symptoms of a cold, hiding the fact that I was just exhausted with *EVERYTHING* that has happened in Uganda so far, and simply wanted to stay in solitude for awhile.

The funny thing was that the doctor just stared at me for what it felt like eternity, perhaps knowing that I was just exaggerating but couldn't decide what to do about it. He paused for some time and finally asked me to just rest and drink more water.

After he left, I knew that I would definitely be alone for the next several hours. I however still couldn't fall asleep. Fine, I told myself, I jumped out from bed and grabbed a book to read.

The book is called "*All God's Children Can Dance*" by Japanese novelist Murakami Haruki. Known for his humorous, surreal style and the capability to capture spiritual loneliness of the modern world, I felt compelled to bring along an anthology of short fictional stories that should match perfectly with the mission's mood and theme.

It was a quick read. It wasn't quite exactly what I have anticipated though. It was a great story, but at a very bad timing.

I read 2 more short stories titled "*Super Frog Saves Tokyo*" and "*Thailand*". Both were figurative with twists that I couldn't relate to the real world with a depleted energy level. I put the book away and lie back down. Suddenly, I felt more lonely than ever before. The insects' buzzing, the muddy smell, and even the sound of my own breathing have all vanished. If I were looking to get something extremely important done, that was probably the best time to do it.

With a sarcastic grin, I closed my eyes and confronted God about the irony He was putting me through.

"So, what's up now? Huh? Okay, let me start in chronological order: first, you let me read about the online ad and gave me all the signs to go ahead with this deal. Then, you have led me jump over the hurdles of fundraising, working with strangers, and non-existent leadership. Next, just when the team and I were getting ourselves psychologically and physically adjusted and settled to the new environment, a conman, a couple of riots, and dozens of sick children all ganged up and paralyzed our plans. And here I am now- freaking half dead just like the other patients at the clinic with little knowledge of when would recuperation take place, if ever. There are literally hundreds of people in the neighborhood that needed help from the outside world, but these is almost nothing we can do to alleviate their suffering. Why are you making everything so tough to those that are willing to serve in your name? Where's the empowerment? I know what you are going to say: it's either 'the purpose for putting people through trial is to build up one's character and perseverance', or 'no one did anything wrong; the reason for all pain and suffering is to glorify my name'. Ha! I don't see how all these would work out at the end. Is this some kind of a joke that you want to play around because you are too bored? Look: we only have about a week to go, and don't tell me you had a long-term plan ahead of us!"

Immediately opened my eyes after completing this "prayer", I waited patiently for my quickened breath and pumped adrenaline to slow down, and to give myself a chance to listen attentively for a response from above.

107

Nothing happened.

Of course. Why did I expect to experience magic so often?

Thanks to this outburst, a "fatigue attack" (I am not sure if there's an official term for such a phenomenon) unexpectedly descended from the top of my head and I collapsed. I did not wake up again until about 5pm. That was 6 hours of quality rest in the middle of the day.

****

Sometimes, when you have the freedom and guts to break away from the habits and routines that were supposed to be the most efficient ways to get through the day, the refreshing feeling that came along could be quite helpful in asking why certain things _have to_ happen a certain way. One example I learned was related to eating 3 meals a day.

I had a light dinner before skipping breakfast and lunch during the day, and "rested" on a bed for no justifiable reason. When I finally woke up, my sore throat, the "clouds in my head", and the bloated belly vanished for yet another unjustifiable reason. I quickly jumped out from bed and walked out of the room to stretch my stiff joints.

The sun was still shining bright, and the guesthouse remained peaceful when I lost consciousness. Since no one was looking, I started doing some jumping jacks and other funny stretching exercises in the middle of the courtyard.

"What are you doing Ambrose?" Will's voice emerged from behind and I almost twisted my shoulder by his unexpected appearance.
"I am just stretching a little. I was sick and slept the whole day." I tried to sound awake and friendly.

Strange enough, Will was getting more motivated: "Do you do these exercises every day?"

"Uh, no, not really, just whenever I feel like it." I continued to swing my arms back and forth, cracking my knuckles, but still couldn't figure out why he was getting excited.

"Ambrose, show us some moves!" Will was getting a little out of control.

"Ugh??"

"Is that real Chinese kung fu? We always watch Jackie Chan's action movies here. We love Jackie Chan!" Will finally solved the mystery, almost too humorously.

"Oh no, no, no… I don't know any Chinese kung fu. My bones were stiff and I needed to shake them off. That's all."

"Can you show us some Chinese kung fu?" Will wasn't listening.

I waved my hands and spoke as loudly as I could: "Those were just movies. I don't have any fighting skills and almost 90% of all Chinese people don't know martial arts, or kung fu of any kind."

That probably stretched a little too far. Will was obviously very disappointed to learn the truth, and kept quiet for a long awhile. Boy, I thought Bruce Lee was the all-time legend, but Jackie Chan seemed to have replaced him in the modern days.

Will didn't go away though. He was still hoping to catch "some moves" live as I wrapped up on the stretching exercises.

The team gradually came back after a day's work, one after the other. Some helped out in the clinic for routine physical

109

checkups on the kids from Dorcas, and some were able to conduct lesson plans like the day before. Things finally started to normalize after almost a week's time.

"You alright now?" Bob saw me and asked.

"Yeah, thank God. I just slept the whole day without eating anything or going anywhere, and I am more refreshed than ever." I skipped the details about the mental battle that really knocked me out.

"That's good. Hey, you want to come with us to Sironko and buy some stuff?"

"Who else is going?"

"Pastor Mick and myself. Will is driving."

"Sounds good." I couldn't wait to just go somewhere and explore.

We took a basket of empty coke glass bottles to a mini-mart and exchanged them for a full load of coke and other soft drinks. We also bought some water and phone cards for the team.

Will took a little detour and showed us the neighborhood. The small town of Sironko had pretty much all the basic stuff like mini convenience stores that sold clothes, food, and hygiene products. Off the main road came a desolated giant mansion that created a sharp contrast against the run-down structures in the area.

Will pointed at that building: "It's the home of a government official."

Just before he made a U-turn and headed back, the car ran into a flock of mosquitoes that looked like dust in the air from a hundred feet away. It wasn't until then I realized that the "few" mosquitoes messing around at Dorcas were truly *nothing*.

Will rolled up and locked all the windows just in time.

By the time we returned to the guesthouse with all the goodies, everyone was in the dining room catching up with each other. Raeanne took a long bike ride with a local doctor deep into the jungle and delivered generic medicines to those that had zero access to medical treatment. Some ladies played guardian angels and reportedly walked more than 70 kids from Dorcas to the clinic and back for physical checkups. Whoever taught had a pretty smooth day with their agendas. It looked like I missed out a lot.

The only person missing was Shirley, and it felt odd without her piercing voice around. Just when I was about to ask for her whereabouts, different conversations converged and became one on the missing person. Pastor Mick, the good jolly fellow, was unusually engaged and took the lead. It wasn't a pretty picture.

The exact details were forgotten, but the lady who suggested the kids could learn to play frisbee because we couldn't readily bring the soccer balls over apparently pissed off more people than I thought. As complaints after complaints from most of everyone surfaced, the fun of gossiping dissipated. The consensus became rather disturbing when nobody could provide a solution.

Frankly, I don't like her either (duh!), but she will be out of my life in a week or so. I doubted that she was a "bad" person by nature, but there were definitely a crap load of sharp, irreconcilable differences sticking out like a sore thumb. I decided to do something meaningful.

"Hmm... you know what, we all came from different backgrounds, and I doubted if anyone on the team in particular wanted to intentionally cause discomfort among others. If that's

111

the case, then it's only a matter of different styles. Remember in Chapter 14 and 15 in the books of Romans where Paul talked about judging other servants? Let's refrain from repeating what had been done in error in the past."

Confession: those weren't the exact wording I used, and I was the biggest hypocrite when I spilled that out.

The crowd did quiet down and some went back to their rooms until dinner was served.

Yes- only one more week left. What's going to happen next?

Well, I miraculously recovered. That was uncalled for, especially after I lost my temper and gave God the middle finger, figuratively.

If the central theme of my faith were genuinely stemmed out of love and grace from above, that was a solid proof.

Let's see what else had been prepared for us in the next 7 days.

From Sympathy (pseudo) To Empathy

Ambrose Tse

Chapter 08: Flight on a Time Machine

Today is dead day for the team, and I personally didn't mind to have another one 2 days in a row.

Because of all the fun we had from the trip to Sironko, Will asked Pastor Mick, Bob, and myself to join him on a half day excursion to "take a look" at the secondary school (or middle and high school in U.S. terms) he used to teach. I assumed "to take a look" meant to chat with the students, prayer walk, and take pictures of the neighborhood. It sounded like a nice break away from the depressing environment, and I had been slacking from what I was initially delegated for: the video and cameraman.

None of us knew that Will taught at a secondary school beforehand. We all thought that he and Liz only co-own and run the daily operations of Dorcas and Shared Blessings, and FCA was their partner that provided the funding. That was partly why Arlene, and the rest of us that tagged along, were treated as honored guests and served with the best accommodations available. The funding had made an obvious impact to both the locals and our hosts. The size of the guesthouse we were staying at plus Will's house were only slightly smaller than the mansion of the government official we saw from a distance the day before. At any rate, Will drove for about half an hour away to the east of town, and stopped at a hilly place with trees and a set of uniformly small brick-like structures built and scattered on a large piece of plateau.

It was a bright and sunny day. I was however pretty sure that it will rain in the afternoon, just like how it had been every day for the last several days. In exchange of the muddy road that took everyone at least twice the time to travel on, the dampness in the air lowered the temperature to a much more acceptable level, or to around the low 80's (28 degrees Celsius in local measurement). Uganda is located right above the equator, so the average temperature during the "normal days" was usually in the high 80's (or about 30 degree Celsius).

115

Will confidently led us through the unidentifiable trestle path to one of the closest building structures. Two men were talking quietly, and Will engaged with them in a what-seemed-to-be-an-everlasting conversation. Meanwhile, I wandered around and took out my camcorder for a round of candid shots of the surroundings.

Thanks to the influence of Lego and my math tutor back in elementary school, I have always been interested in appreciating architectural design, high rises, and constructions, but was never an expert in critiquing them. I could, nevertheless, tell you that different materials were used to construct these comparable "building structures". The newer classrooms in the far right were made up of bricks and cement that looked as solid as a mountain from the outside. The other structures, including the construction right in front, were made of dried mud and rocks, some fortified with long tree branches lined up vertically and horizontally on the outside that functioned as a fence. It was not until later (i.e. after watching Amazing Race) I finally realized that most huts and homes in Africa were made with mud. That was actually pretty smart, being able to use the kind of natural resources they have around them.

Will finally finished chatting and waved at me, and we continued our way onto the school ground. Will explained that those two were his former colleagues, and the students just went back to class after the first morning recess ended. The campus was serenely peaceful. On one hand, the atmosphere reminded me of the quad in the middle of a college campus without the noises. On the other hand, the grassy field needed more flowers or trimmed shrubs badly, as well as other subtleties to sustain the perpetuating ambience.

-Phew-

Hey! What the heck was that thing running through the grasses?!

A dark piece of speckled banner with some bright strips painted on its body swiftly zipped from right to left just a few yards away. The other guys didn't seem to have noticed it. Could it be a squirrel? No, the color didn't match, and that "thingie" didn't dash as agile as a squirrel. Ah! It was a snake! Crap! No, no, no wait- it couldn't be a snake; it was *running* through the grasses. As I panic my eyes continued to curiously search for that "thingie", and it once again whooshed. This time it stopped a couple of feet away to pose for a few seconds, to make sure that I have ample of time to tell what it really was. Ah! It was a lizard! A rare kind too; its head was as ugly and stubborn-looking as all other geckos or turtles, but the color of its skin was awfully attractive. I was frightened as heck, but couldn't take my eyes off of it. These little babies could leap onto the walls and ceilings like Spiderman and extend its footlong curly tongue to seize its delectable prey. And it might become interested to jump onto me and lick my face for a change of taste!

The glamorous but lonely creature quickly moved onto his journey. I swear if he had stayed still a little longer, I would have taken out my camcorder and try to take a quick snapshot. The brownish, murky green ones back at the guesthouse were no competition with this beauty. The skin of this baby reflected a glossy and slimy black highlighted with thick bright yellow stripes like one of my T-shirts. Like charming wild mushrooms, most gorgeous living organisms also come with the most lethal poison ever known to the history of mankind without any antidote. Ironically, any fifth grader could tell you that lizards are indeed our good friend for sweeping out the cunning insects carrying malaria. It was just that the timing was a little off; it showed up when I was dreaming about laying on these quad-like grasslands for a 5-minute sunbathing session. My biggest complaint about them would probably be that they were not eating enough of the mosquitoes.

Hastening my steps to follow more closely behind Will, we soon came to a large, isolated bungalow-type building with some eye-catching features on the façade. The box was made of solid crimson bricks, a large rectangular piece of slanted, rusty metal placed on top as the roof, and window frames painted in baby blue. Baby blue? Yes, that was the charming part. I didn't think it was random though; someone had once said that Africans are pretty big on colors. Each color was supposed to bear a connotative symbolic meaning in terms of social status. But I totally forgot to find out about the details from Will or anyone else afterwards. The 4 of us quickly strode into the room and carried out our little hospitality visit.

Thirty students were seated in a large classroom that still seemed congested with all the wooden furniture organized according to the natural law of entropy. The "desks" were essentially pieces of commercially abandoned elongated wood splinter of different sizes somehow welded together and shared by 2 or 3 students. The most puzzling part was that the benches the students sat on were equally as big as the desks, only built about a foot lower as "chairs". Why couldn't the carpenter make the desks a little wider? Let's see now: I could probably put four pieces of 8.5" by 11" binder papers side by side, and the students could put their arms either under the table or stack them on top of the paper. Okay, I guess these guys here have either learnt to press n' hold a piece of paper with one arm or elbowing each other competitively whenever they need to write.

Evidently, the students have no such problem or whatsoever. And this was like heaven compared to the classroom at Dorcas.

Will murmured a few words with the instructor when we interrupted the class session. He then took over and started talking to the students in an authoritative tone in the local dialect. Another conversation, I meant soliloquy, which seemed to last beyond eternity.

The 3 of us patiently stood and waited for whatever that will happen next. I glanced over to the blackboard behind me and tried to see what lesson the teacher was delivering. Holy crap! It was a list of math equations and problems written in English. Wait a minute: they weren't just math, it's $\mu t + \frac{1}{2}at^2$...hmm...Eureka! These were physics problems that I had so much trouble with back in high school! Wow! The boys were learning the same, difficult stuff like how I used to. Impressive!

After taking a couple of pictures of the class and the blackboard, Will showed no sign of pausing so I continued my observation. The baby blue windows from the far side caught my attention again, but this time it was for a different reason because they looked slightly different than before. I was quite sure that it was the same window I saw from the outside before I walked into this classroom, but something changed. No, it wasn't the angle from where I was looking at, it was more...like the window itself. It wasn't technically a window after all. More precisely, it should be described as a door in the middle of a wall. There was no glass; the "windows" were a solid piece of wooden board painted in baby blue that opened outward primarily as a source for natural lights. Any lizard could easily climb in, and the simple way to avoid this "trivial problem" was to close the window (or door, however you want to define it) altogether.

What's the big deal about this? If you think about it, the pseudo-window defeated the purposes of almost everything a window was supposed to do, and that was only because the glasses were missing. And I failed to mention: there was no light switch in this room either, and this school was *supposed* to cultivate a superior learning environment than most other schools in Uganda, according to Will.

Our tour guide probably noticed my mischievous acts from the students' responses, so he finally ended whatever his was preaching and introduced each of us in English.

"These are our friends from America." Will switched to a softer, slower tone, "They are now teaching and helping out at Dorcas Children Center. There is a total of 12 of them, and 3 came over here today. This is Pastor Mick here to my right, Bob, and Ambrose...."

I put a big old smile on my face and waved. These guys probably understood that an Asian could also be an American, and gave me no special attention.

"And Ambrose knows Chinese kung-fu too!" Will added with exaggerated enthusiasm and a wink towards me.

All the students laughed frantically as I stood dumbfounded. Damn, Will, you just won't believe me, won't you?!

Luckily no one asked me to show him any moves.

"What was that all about?" Bob asked when we stepped out from the classroom.

"I was stretching yesterday after I woke up from a long nap, and Will thought that I was practicing some kung-fu moves like Jackie Chan. But I did tell him that I was only stretching."

"That's funny."

We peeked into a few other classrooms and took more pictures. This was a co-ed school, but the number of girls was highly un-proportional to the number of boys. Before our tour came to an end, we walked by a large piece of flat land made into a soccer field, and Will stopped us and pointed to the players at a distance.

"It's not a P.E. class. These players are practicing to compete in a tournament."

"The World Cup?" Pastor Mick asked innocently.

"Hopefully," Will smiled, "It would be huge if they can represent Uganda."

When we passed by the very last hut (definitely a hut and not any kind of special, undefined building) before making our way back to the car, either Pastor Mick or Bob noticed that it was a worship sanctuary and they asked to take a look at the inside. Will pushed the door and we stepped into a big empty hall.

The hall appeared big and empty not only because there was nobody inside, but also the fact that it did not have much furniture. Not even one single chair or bleacher. Maybe they were shared with the other classrooms?

Equipment and other furnishings up in the front were either broken or crooked, but still useable somehow. While wondering how the worshippers were supposed to carry out services on Sundays, I fell into a trance that took me back to what happened during Christmas week a few months ago. My church at that time was having an outreach program on an evening in the sanctuary and the overhead projector wasn't working properly for some reason. The result? The program ended about 10 to 15 minutes longer than expected, and the crowd got impatient and became critical about the lack of preparations beforehand. The team coordination and transition weren't smooth either, and the gimmick to create a fun, enjoyable evening just wasn't there.

Noises from the conversation between the other guys brought me back to consciousness soon after the flashback ended. My mind went blank as I lifted my head up and saw the crooked cross made from some red cloth and the busy mosquitoes several feet ahead.

****

The ride back to Dorcas felt a lot faster than the ride to the school in the morning, even though it was the exact same bumpy route Will chose. It was a decent, new learning experience, and I got more stuff to add onto my prayer list. The immediate question was: what were we going to do with the remainder of the day? By now, *nobody* dared to say much about generating an agenda of any kind anymore. Yet still, to play by intuition and spontaneity on a daily basis was frustrating, and there was no point in complaining.

I decided to hang around at Dorcas to see what's going on until lunch time. The medical clinic was still a forbidden place to me, but I promised myself to make at least one more visit before we fly back, regardless if it was to help the doctors in however way they wanted, find someone to talk to, or just play with the little patients while they wait to see the doctor.

God, when can I start to focus less on my own feelings?!

The pleasant morning gradually got a lot warmer. The sun pushed the clouds away and transformed the sky into a brighter, bluer skyline that introduced vigor and hope. The team had elected not to hold a class until the following day. Denise, Brenda, and Allison were already running around and got themselves busy with some project.

"Hi everyone! What's going on?"

"Oh hi Ambrose. Haven't seen you this morning until now. What have you been up to?"

"Will took Pastor Mick, Bob, and I to the high school that he used to teach at, and we were given a tour and got to know about the students and their learning environment. We just got back a few moments ago."

"Nice! How was it?"

"It was refreshing. The school is pretty big and the facilities are a lot better than here. But still, they don't have anything extravagant to play with."

"I see. That makes sense. So where are the other guys now?"

"I am not sure. They are probably at the guesthouse meeting with Arlene or something. What are you guys doing here?"

"Nothing much. As you can see, Denise is just kind of babysitting the younger children and make sure no one gets hurt. Allison is somewhere helping the ladies clean up the rooms, and I am trying to finish painting this wall outside of the boy's dorm."

"May I help? I had never ever painted a wall though."

"Sure. It's easy. Make sure you move the brush up and down and be consistent. Put a few extra layers of paint so that it stays on there and make it look rich."

"Okay. Do you have a ladder?" I tilted my head upwards and observed the ten feet wall in front and asked.

"No, but you can use this chair that I was using. Be careful and don't fall. I am going to check out the walls inside." Brenda gave me a few other instructions and let me figure out the rest on my own.

The nature of the job was pretty easy, if you could convince yourself that it was just like painting an oversize picture and be creative like Van Gogh. The problem was the broken seat on the broken chair to be used as a ladder.

How did Brenda stand on this thing?! I looked at the wall and saw that it was about 80% done. The few feet at the top needed some touch up, and that was all.

I searched for a substitute nearby that I could borrow. Nope, nothing like that was within reach. For a split second I thought about asking Denise to lend me her chair, but that would be kind of messed up.

That's alright, I can do it. Let me take a deep breath and think now… I should put the brush in the can and hold the can handle in my left hand first. Then I'll put the chair against the wall and grab onto the right armrest and quickly jump onto the sides of the chair and make myself balance while squatting down. Finally, stand up slowly and start painting!

The strategy worked! Five minutes later, I needed another strategy to come down and move the chair a few feet across to repeat the drill.

God, why does everything have to be that tough?! I could barely paint a wall well even if I had the best tools!

Fine. I will take my time since nobody was rushing me. In fact, I should wait for a few minutes and put another layer of paint until my stiff legs could bend again. That was what Brenda suggested too, right?

So there I stood. The smell of paint thinner mixed with mud was sort of irritating, but at least the mosquitoes have vanished momentarily. On second thought, their disappearance might have more to do with the shining sun, which had been unusually strong within the last hour.

It wasn't really *that* hot. I wasn't sweating yet, but the powerful ray was particularly uneasy on my forehead. It felt like the sun was only shining on a few particular spots directly on my face, and I was sure that I have not fallen sick again. The feeling was uncanny and uncomfortable, no matter how optimistic a person interpreted it.

"Hello, how are you?" I greeted a little boy who suddenly came to my right from nowhere and stared at me.

"You wanna give me a hand?" I tried to sound nice while balancing. I would much rather entertain the children in other ways instead of putting on a circus act.

Nope, no response. My Kiswahili was limited to a few words like "Jambo" (which means hello) or "Malambe".

The boy showed no sign of going away. He was probably only 5 or 6 years old, and wondering what the heck I was doing in that funny posture.

What am I supposed to do now? The worst that could happen was if the kid climb up or punch me in the groin for fun and I fall on top of him. It wasn't funny when I visualize that scene. But I didn't want to just ignore or turn him away either.

Denise went off somewhere and no other adults were in sight. I couldn't shout for help. My legs were starting to numb. Crap.

Before I could come up with something, the boy made his move. He extended one arm and reached for my little black pouch clipped to my waist.

Argh! Don't! My camcorder was in jeopardy!

"No, no, no, no, no, no, please don't touch that thing; it's not a toy!" I shook my head violently.

The smart kid did not appear to understand my exaggerated gestures and kept poking. Talk about being caught between a rock and a hard place.

Alright, I am turning around and getting down with my large and clumsy butt.

Arghhhhhhh! I am falling down!!!!! The can of paint is going to spill all over!!!!!!!!

Nope. Not quite. But this time the boy got scared and walked away. *Phew!!!*

Crack!

Something apparently popped. It was a rare noise, but easy to identify.

The chair was falling apart!

Calm down dude. You were only two feet above ground! I assured myself.

Still, the chance of falling flat on my face was high, and it *will* hurt when none of my hands were free. More importantly, the wall was only 10% done from where Brenda left off!

Okay, I give up. Nobody was present to witness my quandary, and I don't care if someone did see the whole drama and thought that I was a loser.

I took a deep breath and gently "slipped" off the front edge of the chair with my toes pointing towards the ground and landed on the middle of my feet as usual. The chair relieved itself from the intense pressure by immediately collapsing backward to the ground.

Somewhat of a safe landing, I believed. I looked all over and not even single drop of paint was spilled. *Phew!*

I turned around and stepped back to examine the painting of the entire wall. It looked as though the little boy that diverted my attention could have probably done a better job than I did.

Hey, there is a first time to everything! I didn't feel guilty about it.

Brenda would need to pick up after me, obviously, no matter what effort I put in.

The peeled skin on the side of my left index finger, scrapped from somewhere, didn't hurt until I loosened up, and it took forever to heal. I put my thumb on top of it and my right hand to wrap around the left fist. Slowly, the determination to make things better during the remainder of the trip resurfaced, even though I had no idea what that may entail.

It was getting late. I made my way back to the guesthouse for lunch.

****

Mbale, the third largest city of Uganda, was the target destination for the afternoon. It was also the place where Mr. Chauffer stopped and gave us the final break right before we arrived at Dorcas when we were coming in from the airport at the beginning of this exciting adventure. Like any other arrangements, the call to visit the semi-modernized town, initiated by our host, was spontaneous.

Lunchtime was pretty much over by the time I made it back for a quick bite. It was only 1:15pm, but there were only a few dishes of leftovers in the dining room. Will, my other companion who joined me a couple of minutes after I stood next to the serving table trying to figure out what was edible, couldn't figure out what to make do with the limited assortment either. He asked a housemaid to bring him some gravy.

She brought in a can of Campball cream soup.

Will looked disappointed and muttered: "That's not enough gravy…"

"Will," diverting his attention, "Are we doing something special this afternoon?"

"Arlene asked Liz about the possibility of go shopping and get online to send some emails. I think a lot of people are going too."

"May I come along? Is it to Sironko?" I couldn't hide my thirst to touch base with the supporters back home.

"No, we'll take you to Mbale. It's less than an hour away, and there are much more things to shop there than Sironko. We will head off pretty soon, probably right after we finish lunch."

"Okay." I quickly stuffed some food into my mouth and went back to the bedroom to get the list of people that I needed to buy souvenirs for.

Most of the team showed up for this little outing, and Will took the Shared Blessings van to fit us all in. It rained briefly after we hopped into the van, and Will was speeding on the muddy road to get us on our way. Within 45 minutes, we were able to once again see the cluster of buildings and the noises that we have left behind for more than a week.

Certain parts of Mbale, surprisingly, resembled some of the Midwestern town seen in the old cowboy movies. Lots of buildings were made of wood and stood just one story high. The dusty streets were wide enough for a couple of horse carriages to run side by side, and the scorching sun added on to that vivid impression.

Will took us to another part of town first, an area with more traffic, businesses, and high rises (around 4 or 5 stories tall). As the van slipped through herds of vehicles and pedestrians, I took my camcorder out and prepared to take some really candid local shots.

Our very first stop is an internet café named "ASHOK", a place that could satisfy our dying hunger to connect with the virtual world. "Internet Café" was a misnomer; ASHOK was a convenience store selling general local consumer products, imports from Great Britain, and some Indian spices in an aisle or two on the first floor. And if you want to use their internet, go up to the attic on the second floor, and you will find a room with 5 or 5 desktops each with a chair in front. No coffee or any other beverages were served.

Without further ado, the team, including myself, each claimed a throne and logged onto our e-mail accounts as fast as we could. Nobody said anything, and the noise of keyboard-typing had instantly filled the room.

To my disappointment, my inbox only had less than 10 new e-mails, and none of which were really important. At any rate, I thought it would be cool to send someone an email from the middle of Africa. So I wrote a short update to the church fellowship group:

Jambo! (Hi All!)

Just want to drop by a quick note here from Mbale, Uganda. I am having a very blessed time here, although the conditions here are beyond imaginations (more details available when I returned). The children here are very pure, very cute; which requires a lot of faith and courage to serve. Christians here are also very faithful; there is nothing material that they can rely on. I can see the presence of our Lord through them.

I am at a village called Sironko, which is a 40 min. drive from Mbale. There is almost nothing in the vicinity except insects and diseases. But ppl. told me that this is only the tip of an iceberg in Africa. Anyhow, I will come to fellowship on 5/9 with some pics and we can share more later.

Pax, Ambrose

It was an accurate account that sounded positive enough, without distorting any of the conditions worth mentioning. And I kept my friends guessing. Boy, did I not already visualize the kind of popularity I will get once returning, especially with the girls!

The shallow and prideful part of me suddenly took over without any warning.

My fantasy waned within a split second. I moved on to check on the current news on Yahoo, my favorite online portal that also provided free driving directions. Nothing major happened since I left San Francisco, and the rest of the world appeared to be as peaceful, or violent, as usual. The invasion of Iraq was normalizing and major combat had ceased, according to the smartest U.S. president in the entire solar system. The only thing that bothered me the most was the unprecedented chicken flu outbreak in Hong Kong that almost turned the vibrant city into a living hell. I still have a handful of relatives living there. Here in Uganda families with chickens let their pets and babies roam inside and outside of their huts as they pleased.

Our computer session ended voluntarily and amazingly short within half an hour. Liz had to buy some groceries and was checking out on the household and home improvement supplies for Dorcas. Meanwhile, all of us toured around the neighborhood to sightsee and get a feel of what life was like in metropolitan Uganda before sunset.

The sizzling sun calmed down a bit, and it was a comfortable walk. Everywhere was crowded and noisy like any other urban city. The main roads were paved, but the little alleys and marketplaces on the side streets weren't. The mud remained soft and moist from the rain a couple of hours ago, and water was dripping off from almost every canopies.

If you were a thrill seeker and genuinely appreciate culture and diversity, you are in for a treat. Whenever someone walked into one of the narrow alleys off the main street, it was literally another world: a variety of retailers selling clothes, toys, shoes, handyman tools, groceries, cell phones, and any other merchandise you could conceive were mingled with barber shops, tiny snack bars, and broom-making stores on both sides of the alley. The majority of these venues were small, roomy enough to allow one or two persons inside at the most, and the owners made use of the vertical space wisely to store their supplies and products. If not, you would just have to walk very carefully to avoid knocking over any of their protruding inventories. Shoppers were choosing and bargaining, and a few sellers were shouting down the alley to attract the attention of prospects passing by. Of course, being the only Asian looking chubby guy standing in the middle of the marketplace browsing around like a tourist had invited numerous unsolicited offerings. They were aggressive but not effective, since most of them couldn't decide on which language to pitch to me before I passed by them. My appearance had finally given me an edge over some of my teammates, and I was laughing from the inside when I observed from a distance that John, June, and Shirley had to constantly shake their heads and say no to the forceful salespeople.

The fun and chaotic infrastructure of the marketplace implied a subpar standard of sanitary conditions. But seriously, who cares? It was certainly not handicap friendly, and that would be my only concern. It was hard for people in developing countries to take mental note of "trivia" matters of such nature.

Will wanted to show us the nicer part of town after everyone hopped back into the van, and that was where we first came into Mbale, or the quiet cowboy 'hood. The ride was less than 5 minutes long, but it felt like we have traveled to a completely different city. All the roads were cemented and neatly designed so that no one would get lost walking into a smaller street. There were no alleys here. The shops and supermarket were large, sophisticated, and specialized. The district was modernized with trees and other colorful ornaments and structures. Simply put, it wasn't the kind of Africa people would have envisioned.

"Wow, look at those giant TVs!" I looked up as I stopped right outside of an electronic retailer, after realizing that there were no souvenirs I could buy for anyone.

1, 2, 3, 4, 5, 6 zeros… so a 21" tube TV costed more than a million shilling?! I counted the zeros on the price tag twice with my finger and concluded that the TVs were at least a million shilling. How much was that in USD? About $500, if you divide the amount by an even 2,000. Who the heck was going to buy that?! That was like a year's worth of salary for a regular Ugandan worker! And it was a total rip off too; that antique probably cost less than $300 back in the States!

Oh well, why should I be surprised or agitated? It was a luxury on this continent.

After a brief 20-minute walk, Will hurried us back to the van so that we could all return home before the sun sets.

Another valuable experience stored in my piggy bank.

****

The fatigue from hitting 3 different places within a 10-hour timeframe ultimately melted down onto my shoulders and knees when I sat down in the dining room for a "brief" meeting that Arlene called upon before dinner.

Tipping, Arlene announced, was the topic of discussion for the night. Let's come up with a decision together before Liz and Will come in for dinner about an hour later.

Tip who? Arlene explained that the extra housemaids who had been cooking and serving all the meals since we arrived were actually transferred from Dorcas, and in return Liz let them consume the dinner leftovers for their work. We, as a team, should show our appreciation by giving them some tips, including the maids that were originally here (i.e. Agnes, the girl who brought Will the can of gravy earlier during lunch).

Okay, I was all for it. The budget for lodging was left unused, so we had plenty to give out. How much and how should we give the tips out without making our host look bad?

And this was the best part of the discussion.

For the next 45 minutes, each person presented a different opinion and at the end, nothing had been decided.

I sat there and listened and waited and listened and waited and listened, and have determined that going forward, I will no longer depend on or be influenced by any of these folks. The arguments went back and forth and the gibberish was ludicrous, no matter how you look at it.

So what now, God? It's just between you and me. What will the next few days look like?

No answer, as usual.

Fine. I was too tired to do anything anyway. As soon as dinner was over, I sprinted back to the bedroom and knock myself into a coma after recording what happened today in my diary.

But right before I finished writing, Pastor Mick came in for a small chat.

"How was your day?" I asked.

"Good, very eventful. I think both of us can agree on that."

That was the first comforting joke I heard for today, at 10pm.

"Do you know that Bob moved out and now it's just you and me staying in this room?"

"Really?!" I was, frankly, quite surprised, "Since when? No wonder it looked like there was less stuff lying around on his bed. Did he say why?"

"No, and those are my stuff on that bed. But I am going to sleep on my own bed anyway. More space for us both, I don't care."

If I were Pastor Mick, I would put my luggage onto Bob's bed too. His bed was kind of like a jail cell. But the fact that Bob didn't tell us that he was moving out ahead of time was somewhat out of the ordinary. Yet like what Pastor Mick said, I didn't care either.

"Good night Pastor Mick, oh…" I woke up from my digressed thought, only to find that Pastor Mick had already gone to bed.

Geez, he could fall asleep and start snoring in no time!

After turning the light switch off, I began to reflect on the different little things that had taught me about humanities and cultures. When I thought I finally had some peace and quiet to dive deep into contemplation, I immediately fell asleep like Pastor Mick.

Four hours later, or after my first cycle of rapid eye movement (or "REM") was completed, I could no longer stay in bed and pretend nothing happened. Deep in my soul I knew that I must do something to make sure that my time here in Uganda would be worthwhile. I got out of bed, quickly climbed down from the bunk beds, and rushed to the outside and took a deep breath to yawn as silently as I could. I cared less if there were a lion waiting right outside of the bedroom. The agony was just too much.

Pastor Mick was showing off his magical tricks in his sleep again!

Chapter 09: Behind the Scene Special Feature

It was time to get those lazy bones back to work.

The back-to-back time off was refreshing but a little too relaxing. The quality of sleep from the prior night wasn't superior. During breakfast I convinced myself to give the best I could to work for the kids.

"It's Labor Day today, so there won't be any formal classes held at Dorcas. But if any of you want to go there and do something fun with the children, please go ahead." A female voice from behind gave me a slap on the face almost instantly.

That's alright; I *will* go play with the kids and hang out there all day. Something good will happen. I have faith that God will provide that opportunity.

Sometimes, making little optimistic statements like this at the beginning of the day could boast morale that would make a real difference during the day, regardless of the outcome at the end of the day. This is one of those corny ideas that we knew well, nodded, but never put in practice. And I will, at least for today, if not more.

Allison, Brenda, and I walked together to the children center on another beautiful morning after a swift breakfast. The muddy road dried up for an easy walk, but it still took a good 5 minutes to get to Dorcas. While the 3 of us were talking about the random things we saw in Mbale from yesterday, a few boys suddenly ran into us before we got to the intersection and held tightly onto our arms.

"Tid-chaer! Tid-chaer!" These kids were chanting these words as they looked into our eyes, determined.

137

"Hey, what happened?" I thought something bad might have happened and these boys were looking for some adults for help.

None of the boys grabbed our arms and dragged us forward. Instead, each of them slid their hands into out palms and held on firmly as we all walked towards Dorcas. They continued to look into our eyes and smiled.

I stood in awe. The very next second I smiled back, and the 6 of us spent one of the warmest moments in life until we reached Dorcas.

****

No matter how other people diplomatically labeled Dorcas, it was a place that hosted dozens of orphans that needed both physical and spiritual nourishment. I would of course still refer Dorcas as a children center in the public, not because I didn't want to get bashed, but more because of the reality that most people in the first world countries just couldn't understand the urgency of the word "orphans" implied without first-hand experience. It would only make matters worse if anyone wanted to shove a new idea onto someone else.

The national holiday created little difference at Dorcas. In fact, more works needed to be done to accommodate the unattended children. That's good! Let's be creative and play by the ears!

To my dismay, the ladies took the risk of getting robbed and brought a small bag of arts and craft supplies for a rather low key but imaginative session. No scissors, just the simpler tools like glue, crayons, bits and pieces of paper stars, and a stack of precut heart-shaped colored papers. About 15 young boys and girls gathered around a table as Allison and Brenda took out the instruments and showed them what they could make from these simple ingredients.

And thank goodness, activities like this did not appeal to a large crowd. The older kids went off to either play soccer or some other games.

Mini Beyonce and Alan were among the 15 students. Mini Beyonce stopped dancing and became an attentive audience for the little project she had committed while ignoring my greeting. Alan, on the other hand, recognized me and smiled back.

Once again, even without an interpreter, Brenda communicated effectively and captured the spectators' attention. The kids each took a piece of the pre-cut paper and either drew something or glued the tiny stars onto it. I looked into the bag and see what other gadgets were buried in there.

There were a couple of frisbees hiding. Yes, the ones that Shirley suggested to bring for recreational bonding times with the older kids, in lieu of the soccer balls. Bob was still holding onto them until the right timing to be suggested by Liz.

The art class was progressing satisfactorily without any uproar. I took off and explored what else was going on. If there were enough kids hanging around without much to do, I will try to show them how to play with these disks, even though I had never learnt how to throw or catch them correctly. Let's just say it'll be a learning process for everyone, shall we?

I've gotten some boys' attentions as soon as I pulled one yellow and one neon green frisbee from underneath my shirt and flashed them in the air. They were coming at me to check out the toy, but I waved and signaled them to move away. Befuddled, a couple of boys stopped where they were and I swung my arms to let go of the yellow frisbee.

Please note: I didn't "throw" the frisbee; that "thingie" escaped from my stiff sticky fingers and flew to my right, about 10,000 feet away from where it was supposed to land.

Obviously, no one caught it. But a few rushed over and took possession of it.

The winner picked up the frisbee and flipped it, knocked and pressed on it, and appeared to have as much fun just to examine the new toy.

When they were finally done checking it out, one of them also swung his arm and let go of the frisbee. It went to his left, and the small crowd was cheering and got super excited for some strange reason.

Oh great, they thought that's how the game was supposed to be played!

It wasn't like I didn't want to show them the right way, but I seriously sucked at it. How do you know when to let go? Should you toss it at waist level or higher? When people first introduced to me in college that ultimate frisbee games were popular and regularly held on campus, I had a hard time withholding my laughs.

What the heck, as long as they had fun, what did it matter?

I played dumb and rushed over as quickly as I could and picked up the frisbee to repeat the drill. I didn't swing my arm as hard this time, and the frisbee floated in the air quite smoothly and landed perfected into the arms of the intended recipient.

"Finally!" I couldn't subdue my elation. It was a perfect throw from my long-gone dexterous instinct!

The boy who accidentally grabbed the disk appeared miserable. His facial expression told me that he believed he had made a mistake. He stood there and paused for a long time. A taller boy came by and snatched the frisbee and threw it back at me. This time, the frisbee hit the ground much sooner, bounced and rolled on its side for several yards, and gradually stopped a few feet away from where I stood.

"Huh?" It was my turn to become befuddled. None of the boys looked mad or disgusted. But they were just as confused as I was.

Nope, couldn't figure out what the heck was going on. I picked up the frisbee and purposely threw it all the way up into the sky to buy time for some analysis.

Before anything remotely sensible popped into my mind, an unexpectedly loud cheer broke out when the frisbee dropped to the ground and rolled in circles after traveling 10,000 feet in the air. A group of kids were racing to the destination to compete for the prize, and they were having so much fun navigating through the process.

Oh, I get it! It was totally my fault. The time when I flung the disk properly and the boy caught it properly, it disrupted their initial perception. Chasing around the toy like a soccer ball was what they preferred!

Argh, what the heck, this was the best that could be done without a translator around. In the beginning I was fantasizing on setting up some ultimate game that a large co-ed crowd would enthusiastically compete for.

I didn't dare to bring out the neon green frisbee to further complicate things.

After putting up with this exhilarating game for about 5 more minutes, all of the boys, one by one, woke up to their senses and pursued a brighter future. They went back to play with the old soccer ball. Being a classical opportunist, I put the frisbees back in the duffle bag and followed the crowd.

What a ludicrous flop.

I watched from a distance the immense zeal infecting every player on the field, including those who chased from behind and never actually get to kick the ball. It wasn't difficult to understand the fever this sport had brought all over the world since the beginning of time. It might not be as fun to watch the professionals pass the ball back and forth for 90 minutes in a game on TV, but the energy and roughness proliferated into the atmosphere would capture everybody's attention.

The soccer ball these kids were playing wasn't technically a "ball". It was made up of layers of worn woven cloth wrapped around and around several times. I guessed the ball was sturdy enough and worked fine as a substitute, but I would need to remind Bob to hand those out so that I could see them play with the real ball at least once before our departure.

Speaking of Bob, I saw him during breakfast but didn't have the chance to ask him about his new accommodation. He never brought it up, so I didn't bother to ask.

Before returning to the playground, I checked on the arts and crafts class and it looked like all the students were almost finished. Each were showing off his or her piece of heart to the adjacent neighbor with the glued glittering stars and the word "Jesus" written in the middle. I took my camcorder out and snapped a picture of a girl holding up her masterpiece.

Did they know what it meant?

Maybe, maybe not. But who cares? They had fun. I hoped they won't misplace their little artwork by mistake too soon.

The growing restless crowd was shouting in excitement and I couldn't help but rushed to see what was going on. The boys seemed to have organized themselves into 2 teams and got a game going. The same behavioral patterns continued: when one player took control of the ball, all other players, except the goalies, would chase after the ball and try to get a piece of it until someone kicked it out of bounds. Then, the process repeated again after the throw in, or until someone scored.

Ten minutes passed by, and the 2 teams remained tied. Suddenly, Jon and Mark, the 2 young British guys working for our host, came out from nowhere and took over the field. The players didn't appear to care about the intrusion and moved to the other side of the boy's dorm and continue to kick around.

"What the …?" I stepped forward to question the validity of the infringement.

Before I get in front of either one of them, a group of smaller kids came out and Jon was holding the hands of two kids and yelled "Let's make a circle!" while leaping around in a big circle on the soccer field. A dozen other kids joined in and hopped like everyone else. Mark, the cooler and skinnier of the 2, stood on the other side and observed.

I rarely bumped into them in the guesthouse ever since one of them handed us the key to our bedroom when we checked in, not to mention holding just a casual conversation. The last time we met was when we were at the courtyard talking about random things and the 1990 World Cup for a brief moment. From what I was told, they were in college and took an academic leave to come to Uganda for a few months to volunteer and experience life. To me, they seemed to have worked at Dorcas for a pretty long time already.

Flare of laughter and screams of ecstatic joy sprung from that "circle" every now and then, and it was a common scene at any elementary school during its recess time.

Remembering the "pledge" I made a few hours ago, my ambition to create and experience the so-call "make today the best day" had returned. When the crowd disbanded to take a break for the mid-morning snack (the murky brown cup of beverage), I sprinted to the playground and picked up a toddler, stretched my arms as far as I could, raised her up, spun around in circles, and shouted "You are a big kid now!!!!!"

Horrible mistake.

"You really shouldn't have done that," replied Jon, when I later recited to him what happened, "I did that once also and all the kids ganged up on me."

For a moment I worried that the erratic attack might have scared the little girl, or if I was making her dizzy with the spin and howling. But she put on the sweetest smile and seemed to be contented with some crazy stranger playing with her like that. As I started to feel a bit dizzy myself, I slowed down and put her back on the ground. The whole process took less than 20 seconds.

The cute smile on that girl's face vanished quickly, but she didn't extend her arms or ask for more. She walked away slowly and quietly. It was short, but I knew she had fun.

My dizziness also went away quickly. More kids saw what happened and gathered around me for some hugging and play time. The self-inflicted popularity didn't excite me though, especially when the assembly got bigger and bigger and the scene reminded me of the candy riot.

I picked up another boy for the same set of exercises. The larger crowd, consisted of about 5 or 6 toddlers, didn't make me nervous either. It wasn't like I invented a game or had anything particularly invigorating to offer. Why would the children get all pumped up over it?

Pop!

"Oh crap! My knees-" I almost collapsed and bite my tongue just when I tugged my hands under the boy's armpits and lifted him up for takeoff.

That kid was, from rough eyeballing, at most 5 years old; and he weighted at least 50 pounds!

He had the abnormally large worm-filled belly just like every other kid here at Dorcas, but the weigh didn't come from there. It was, let me recall… came from pretty much every part of his whole body. I ain't no doctor, but my gut feeling told me that these kids' physicality was inherently brawny.

I took a deep breath and grabbed the boy again to lift him up as high as I could. Damn, it hurt more than doing repetitive bench press in the gym.

The boy put on a sweet smile too like the last girl, apparently less energetic. My arms began to shake after 10 seconds or so, and I had no choice but to put him back on the ground.

"*Hey what the-*" I almost couldn't find a spot to let go of the boy safely. Over two dozen kids surrounded me and yearned for the same ride!

"No, no, no, no, no, no, I am very tired already. Sorry." I kept shaking my head and waved my hand and searched for a way out.

The pleading and teary eyes from the toddlers wouldn't give up easily. Some stretched their arms, roared out some words, and begged for a chance to play the human swinging game.

Frustrated with the helpless situation, I swung my arms wide and in a coarse voice screeched: "NO! I said NO! Okay?! Leave me alone!"

I sounded irritated enough that the group dispersed in an instance. What bothered me the most was, among all the personal issues I had to subsequently deal with, that none of the kids left with signs of disappointment. Being refused was natural to them.

I limped back with the popped knee to the empty arts and crafts table where the class had already been dismissed. I immediately regretted on being a hot temper jerk. Sure, the low energy level and my underestimation on the overwhelming response was part of it. But why did I give the children some hope only to take it back right away?

Calm down loser, calm down. There must be something else underneath this whole mess. I would need to figure them out before I take action next time. Otherwise, I would never get anything done within the next few days before we leave. The clock is ticking faster now.

For almost 15 minutes I sat on one of the broken chairs that still supported my weigh. The mosquitoes were smart enough to leave me alone during this time, and so were the kids. A few of them were lingering around but ignored me. I closed my eyes for some reflection time.

No voices yet. I was glad that I didn't fall asleep. But the mixed emotion hadn't been sorted out yet.

Damn, I needed a counselor badly. But who was available? Could I rely on anyone on the team?

Heck no. That's out of the question, and I was not shy to admit that.

The noise level remained about the same, with occasionally screaming from kids playing their self-invented games.

My meditation / prayer continued: *God, why did you ask me to come all the way to Uganda? Is it only to fulfill my ego so that I can impress everyone I know that I went to an orphanage in the middle of a jungle?*

Or, if you sincerely wanted us to help the neglected and marginalized, where is the help?! How do you expect us to work the problems out if we didn't even have access to the proper tools to work with, like a normal chair, some locals we could communicate with, or even just food that could nourish us rather than mosquitoes that bite us? I didn't quite mind the conman and the leader that never communicate with the rest of the team, but do you know how horrible it felt to see people suffer and there was absolutely <u>nothing</u> you could do about it other than just sit there and watch?! If these orphans were meant to be born, get sick, and die in a matter of only a few years, why were they conceived in the first place? Why should anyone even care about their existence? Where is your love? Answer me God!

This accusation was by far the most succinct and organized outcry that I had ever dared to put forth. It was all completed in one undisrupted thought.

Drops of sweat were covered all over my forehead. Unlike last time, I didn't fall into a coma. I sat there in a fixed posture with my eyes wide opened, numbed to the bone.

None of the activities paused during my meditation / reflection time. In fact, it got nosier when Jon and Mark returned for another round of a different game. This time, it involved a small group of boys where they folded some paper airplanes and set to launch them on the playground.

"1, 2, 3- fly!" Jon whistled the command to see which airplane could go the farthest. Ironically, each and every one of them made a sharp turn downward within a few feet and fell to the ground within seconds.

Another round of laughter broke out.

Nothing was actualized from this set of observations. I turned around and searched for other thought-provoking occurrences, whatever they might be.

The few kids that were lingering near the arts and crafts table showed no sign of switching to a bigger area for their game. A little boy was singled out, and he put little hands together, eyes closed, praying earnestly and silently about something with a very serious face.

I walked up to him, and a series of Bible verses from the gospel of Mathew came to mind:

"Therefore I tell you, do not worry about your life, what you will eat or drink; or about your body, what you will wear. Is not life more important than food, and the body more important than clothes? Look at the birds of the air; they do not sow or reap or store away in barns, and yet your heavenly Father feeds them. Are you not much more valuable than they? Who of you by worrying can add a single hour to his life?... if that is how God clothes the grass of the field, which is here today and tomorrow is thrown into the fire, will he not much more clothe you, O you of little faith?... but seek first His kingdom and His righteousness, and all these things will be given to you as well. Therefore do not worry about tomorrow, for tomorrow will worry about itself. Each day has enough trouble of its own."

I looked up into the sky and there were no birds. I looked onto the playground and it was all mud. Then I looked at the boy in front of me, and he hadn't stopped praying.

Everyone at Dorcas was not faring well, but well above my expectations, because there was nothing they need to compare themselves with. The only fundamental question remained: "Why the heck am I here?"

****

Zzzzzz....is my favorite pastime next to eating.

God knew how many hours had elapsed before I returned to the bedroom for some quality rest. The skipped lunch had no adverse impact to my sound rejuvenation. It was already 4pm by the time I stepped back into the dining room for some socializing, and a group of women were chatting and laughing in Denise's bedroom.

"Oh hi, what's going on?" I trashed my courtesy and interrupted the women talk.

"Oh hi Ambrose, did you just wake up?" Denise probably saw my hairdo and didn't mind the rudeness.

"Yeah. What are you ladies doing?"

"We're making some arts and crafts with the leftover scraps of papers and whatever else we still have. You want to join?"

"Sure!" Allison and Brenda were the other two in the room. I wondered if there will ever be a chance the mix would be different, like me and Shirley passionately working on something together.

Extreme sarcasm there.

"What's this piece of pink "curtain" hanging over your bed?" I pointed to the thin see-thru cloth that couldn't ensure any privacy.

149

"This is the mosquito net Liz gave us", explained Denise, "Can't live without it. Don't you guys have one in your room?"

"No, we just wear long-sleeves shirts and pants when we go to bed. It was bearable, and I will pass on the pink color."

"This thing worked fine though, and they only cost $4. Sometimes, charitable organizations just gave them away to homes, especially to women".

"How come I haven't seen them around?"

"That's because they sell them and use the money to buy food and other things, sadly."

"Oh…" I sighed.

We moved on to the handiwork and kept quiet for a moment. Soon, another round of conversation took off.

"So, we haven't talked about this yet, and it's something pretty basic. What made you join this trip?" Allison threw out this question and hoped that someone would catch it.

I wanted to be a listener first on this.

Brenda broke the brief moment of silence: "Back in fall of last year I was looking at an opportunity to go on an overseas mission trip but couldn't decide on where to go or what God wanted me to do. I waited for some kind of a signal, but there hasn't been any for a long time. Just when I was about to give up, one day at a church service a guest speaker came and talked about the different places he had done ministries in. I paid careful attention and he specifically mentioned the country of Uganda. Then, I went back to my notes and found this opportunity. Everything went pretty smooth after I have confirmed that this is the trip that I should go."

"Wow, that's kind of how I end up joining this team!" Either Allison or Denise commented.

Each of them then shared their stories concisely. I didn't, because there was no point repeating the same stuff over and over again. Luckily, they didn't push for it either, and we happened to finish wrapping up the conversations as well as the arts and crafts stuff right before dinner time.

****

Pastor Mick called for a brief worship time / devotion / informal sharing meeting in the gazebo after the meal, something that was nostalgic since rehearsing for the opening ceremony on day number two. Everyone showed up promptly for this long-forgotten event.

Pastor Mick played the guitar as loudly as he could, and we spent a quick 10-minute singing some old familiar hymns to boost our spirit up and bring back the mojo. When the music stopped, I looked around and saw signs of relief from the faces of many. I was taking some deep breathes happily as well.

Pastor Mick then read a scripture from the Bible, preached a little bit, and asked us to ponder on the meaning of it. Next, he split the 12 of us into 4 groups of 3 for some sharing time. The request was unexpected: we were asked to each share our personal salvation testimony. I first thought it was a little out of line, but on second thought this was also something that we should have done even earlier. The good part was that he didn't tell us *not* to share other things related to this trip if we wanted to. The only troubling part was to do this with two other randomly selected members.

Phew! After some really random methods, my partners for the evening happened to be Raeanne and Pastor Mick, who were sitting next to me. How lucky.

151

"So, how are things in the clinic? I haven't been back since the first day because I couldn't see how I can help as a layman." I initiated the dialogue and directed the question to Raeanne.

"It was okay," Raeanne answered slowly and carefully; "We got a lot done, especially in helping the doctors to get the tools and medicines they needed to treat the patients. We examined all the Dorcas kids and made sure that each and every one of them weren't suffering from any life-threatening diseases."

"That's wonderful news!" I exclaimed.

"Yeah, and if you want, you can always come to the clinic just whenever. There's always something a healthy person can do."

"Of course, I planned to swing by at least one more time before the last day." I smiled back.

Pastor Mick starred at me with half of his eyes closed, emotionless.

"Okay, Ambrose, would you like to tell us how you have decided to accept Jesus Christ as your personal savior?" PM took over with a terse intervention.

"Sure. I will be brief: there wasn't any one particular incident that caused me to make that decision. I was born into a Christian family in Hong Kong and had a pretty decent life up until when the 4 of us immigrated to San Francisco more than a decade ago. We had to start our livelihood from scratch and there had been a lot of trouble adjusting to a new life in the U.S., not to even mention about the financial side of things. I remembered we used to have only one dish to share among the 4 of us for dinner, and that was carrot and chicken. It is a very healthy dish and could be a tasty one too, had we put the right source to cook the chicken with. But the bottle of sauce sometimes cost more than the meat itself, so we used to have very bland food. This was only one of the many rather trivial unpleasant experiences, but my point is that I had a lot of grievances and never understood the kind of, for a lack of a better word, crap that I had to go through when a loving God seemed to have just suddenly exited from my life for no good reason. During my teenage years I have said and done a lot of different things to defile God, but at the same time I really wanted to go back to Him and asked all kinds of questions. It was a strange feeling, but by the time I got to college, I have finally found the time to sit down and think about my life. I have still yet to understand the "whats" and "whys", but I have decided to work with God and see what He will do about my life. So here I am, still stubbornly meandering through the different adventures. It wasn't exactly a rosy picture, but that's my story."

Pastor Mick and Raeanne kept on listening attentively after I stopped talking. Then both of them realized that I finished sharing and woke up from a daze.

"Wow, that's quite something, especially on the part about the sauce and the chicken" replied Raeanne, "My story is very different: it had to do with drugs and several romantic relationships in my 20's. But I see how we are the same when we wanted to have God back into our lives and reconciled with Him."

Raeanne then gave us some details about her journey, which made me realize that my "tragic" past was not entirely comparable to hers. Hers was truly rocky, but she hung on and never gave up her faith. Humble bow to her.

Pastor Mick called times up when it was his turn to share, citing that it was getting late. I stared at him but he didn't escape from my frown. I guess he really didn't expect anyone to expect him to share. Well, our group have had enough sharing.

It was an eventful but satisfying day, one of the few that I wished to recur, if I had enough time to sort out the lessons learnt and connect the pieces.

The groups wrapped up the evening with a prayer, and PM quietly murmured to Arlene that he had an opening for someone to hold morning devotion on the last day before heading out to the airport, and he didn't really want to fill in himself. As a skillful eavesdropper, I had an illogical urge to volunteer.

"Oh good! Basically, you pick a scripture from the Bible and it can be anything you believed worth sharing based on those verses. Open us with a prayer, share, and close. That should take about 15 minutes altogether. Sounds good?" PM was relieved.

"There shouldn't be a problem." I answered succinctly.

After changing into pajamas, I flipped through the pages in the Bible and searched for a meaningful scripture that can relate to a story that I personally wanted to talk about. It wasn't as easy as PM put it, and the whole devotion will be restrained to 15 minutes on everyone's empty stomach. And when I told PM yes, I forgot one important thing: I have never led devotion before.

This was just great. Where did that sudden illogical urge come from?

I will figure something out.

From Sympathy (pseudo) To Empathy

Chapter 10: A Belated PTO

"You are not serious, are you?" I was stunned at the news Bob brought back.

"Yup, we are all going out for a break for the day." Bob confirmed.

"Didn't we just have one not too long ago?" I meant to say yesterday.

"I guess Arlene wanted everyone to take a break and go as a team, and it was Liz's idea since there isn't much left to do. Plus, this place we are going is a very famous tourist spot worth visiting."

Well, that's good; at least there would be a platform for some internal communications. I was not too sure about the "not much left to do" part.

After a hasty breakfast everyone, including Will and Liz, took a car and a van and started to venture out. That did remind me, after all, that Doctor Doug and Raeanne did not go to Mbale or any other places outside of Sironko with the majority of the team. Raeanne, however, briefly mentioned that she did ride on the boda boda, or the back of a bicycle, to a remote village about 10 miles deep into the forest to help take care of the direly sick folks that couldn't make their way out to see a doctor in town. Someone somehow managed to hook her up with this day-long memorable project that wasn't elaborated quite enough, until I personally found out more about it later.

That happened on the day when Will had mistakenly identified me as a kung fu master when I was pulling my groin muscles after falling into the first long coma.

This place we were heading to was called "Sipi Falls"; supposedly one of the astonishingly breathe-taking waterfalls in

Uganda according to the travel guide I bought from the bookstore chain. If anyone were on his or her way for a hiking trip in Mount Elgon National Park, this place near the border of Kenya is a must-see. Fortunately, it was only 4 miles away from where we stayed. Unfortunately, it was four miles going uphill on mostly dirt road. It took us quite some time to get there. Plus, Will stopped at a few Kodak spots for us to take pictures along the way.

It was perhaps still a bit too early in the morning. Interactions between anybody were minimal. I was sitting at shotgun in the van again and no one complained. I turned around and saw that everyone pretty much sat in the same seats as before. It seemed like they became fairly comfortable in their own territory.

Will pulled over at a stop on a hill just 10 minutes after we got into the car to let us get off and stretch. If I remembered correctly, it was either Doctor Doug or John who pulled a muscle and needed to shake things off. For me, it was also a perfect time to step away from the crowd after chucking all the food within 5 minutes during breakfast.

After coughing real loud to cover up and finish the urgent business, I walked towards the cliff and took a good glance of rural Uganda below. It was another perfect day with lots of sunshine and little overcast, with some gentle breeze blowing every now and then. It will get scorching hot in a few hours, then it will pour like cats and dogs in the late evening before you knew it. Another typical day during the rainy season in Uganda.

Whatever things turn out to be, the beautiful scenery totally captured my attention. I honestly thought about spending a few good hours by myself sticking around here instead of going to Sipi Falls. I imagined any views from an elevated point would give people a strange feeling of superiority, regardless if it were a blend of skylines made up of high rises or simply a plain piece of land. The travel guide wrote about how more than 75% of the population lived in the suburbs and on subsistence farming, yet everywhere I saw was empty green pastures with some huts and trees that were miles apart. Well, what did I know about how farmland *ought* to look like. But boy, did they not look like those Lego pieces and model homes I used to play with, and the tranquility was unsurpassable.

"Alright, let's get going now!" Someone yelled from behind and crushed my short-lived fantasy.

The cars kept moving onto the winding uphill roads and passed by a few huts that put up a large sign in the front that offered lodging for one U.S. dollar a night. It seemed like we were getting closer to a tourist destination, and some thrill seekers have definitely taken the risk of staying in a hut far from any community before embarking their hiking journeys in Mount Elgon National Park. Without further ado, the vehicles stopped in front of a wooden structure, what seemed to be an informal visitor information center, and a restaurant behind it.

"Isn't it too early for lunch??? And where's Sipi Falls???" I thought to myself.

The group slowly and susceptibly marched inside, and it had become evident that the establishment was in fact a very decent recreational lodge / pub designed for foreigners. On and around the reception desk were some brochures and souvenirs lined up for review or purchase, and a large foos ball table was placed in the middle of the dining room right around the corner. Several chairs and tables were organized and placed against a set of glass windows, which provided direct access to the balcony. That was an excellent place to appreciate the beauty of Sipi Falls from a few miles across.

Sipi Falls, by all standards, is nothing comparable to, say, the Niagara Falls, but it has its charm. If anyone bothered to google the images of the landmark, you can see that the one-stream fall looked like a giant peeing from above. What's attractive were the rocks behind and the green around the waterfall, which made the little stream all the more precious pouring from a small outlet in the middle of a mountain.

I took a few shots of this magnificent view and checked out the surrounding areas from afar. They were almost identical to the views noted earlier: trees and huts were sprawled on pieces of large green pastures, with the exception that the hills added depth to the imagery and made it more interesting to search for anything that appeared out of the ordinary, such as an extra small, undiscovered waterfall hiding behind some tree to the left of the main fall. Sipi Falls was reportedly made up of 3 different segments originated way up from the north.

Nothing like that was spotted. After a brief moment I turned around and went back inside to see what else was going on. A group of British travelers was sitting at a small table not far from ours and engaged in some exciting conversation in barely audible voices. They were drinking some local beer but weren't talking enthusiastically.

I walked back out to the entrance and tried to explore the vicinity. Nothing interesting there either, but the van we were in caught my attention. It was an old white Japanese mini cargo van refurbished into a 10-passanger minivan, with curtains hanging inside and an extra mirror installed at the back on the outside for parking purposes. Supposedly, there was nothing interesting there either, but minivans of these styles remained me of the ones I saw in the mid 1980's in Asia, and I wondered how old this vehicle really was.

I walked to the driver's side and found the readings of the odometer- 5, 3, 1, 2, 5, 8- this old van had been driven for over half a million miles and still running?!

Wait- something must be wrong; shouldn't the reading be 53,125.8 instead? But that can't be true either. The last digit didn't seem to be a decimal point, and the van would be too beat up for this little mileage.

Hmmm… Ah ha! I see what happened; it was a Japanese import, and everywhere outside of the U.S. uses the same measuring system, which is the metric system! The unit of measure must have been kilometers rather than miles, which would give me… let's see now… one mile is equal to one point six kilometers, which means that 500,000 kilometers would give at least…hmmm… 300,000 miles?!

This is an old van regardless what measuring system was used. It was still working fine. If not, with the "help" from me and Pastor Mick, this little toy would have broken down a long time ago.

I was amazed at its durability. I bet you that all these other white vans on the road, which made up at least 50% of all traffic, were probably even more worn out, given how there were always at least 20 passengers jam packed inside.

A fat hen sauntered right in front of the van and leisurely approached to the corner of the bottom of a fleet of steps, with four of its infants waiting. For a split second I had the evil thought of getting extremely close to their nest and pick up "something" to see how they would respond, but the very next moment I stopped. The footstep of a few other pedestrians emerged, and I looked up.

"What are you looking at, Ambrose?" asked Allison, softly.

"These chickens here. I wondered how each household always raise a family and just let them roam around in the open, without a cage or anything. But at the end of the day, these poultry could find their way home." It was an honest speculation that stopped the mischievous idea from being carried out.

161

"Yeah, they can probably sell the eggs and they provide a stable source of income."

I stood back up and saw June, Shirley, and Raeanne talking to one of the British travelers sitting not far from our table. Her outfit suggested that she was in her early 20's and ready to conquer Mount Kilimanjaro.

That was almost correct. She and a few friends just finished a project in Kenya and were on their way for a hiking trip in the Democratic Republic of Congo. But they have heard that rebel fighting had escalated, and it just wasn't that safe to even get close to the western border of Uganda. They stopped advancing and decided to hike the less challenging Mount Elgon National Park.

The gal took off as soon as she finished talking and all of us returned to the lodge and ordered some refreshments.

The menu was pretty comprehensive: the restaurant offered some western food like sandwiches and fries as well as some local favorites like matoke. I wanted neither, seeing that they have something called chapatti, or an Indian snack like a hybrid of crepe and naan bread.

"Will, may I order this?" I pointed at the menu item to make sure no misunderstanding occurred.

"Yeah, we'll be ordering this for everyone. I don't think we have made this dish for you yet. It's good. It's like some thin and chewy Indian bread without yeast, and it's difficult to make. Anything to drink?"

The mini drink menu on the table offered something more appealing than the usual Coke, Sprite, and Fanta Orange: it's the unique Sarsae. This was something like root beer with an herbal twist to it. I have tasted this in Southeast Asia before, but didn't know it was also available in Africa.

"May I get a bottle of Sarsae?" I asked Will.

"Oh yeah, this is something special and local."

Our food and drink were served quickly and I took a sip of the dark brown Sarsae.

It was root beer, no doubt.

I examined the bottle carefully and saw a totally different name: something about honey water on the body, with the Coca Cola Company label printed towards the bottom.

The waiter also brought out some matoke, rice, and beans, along with some smoky chapatti. Yum... it was a carb-ful festival, and nobody would go hungry for the rest of the afternoon for sure.

Being the honorable host, Will put a little bit of everything on the plate and served everyone.

Vowed to never waste any food, I swallowed all the other filling stuff before I set to enjoy the piece of warm chapatti all by itself at the end.

Will was right this time. This piece of sturdy bread was nothing like crepe but more like naan, except that it tasted better. The texture, the crisp on the burnt parts, and the wheat aroma could literally make me eat this for breakfast, lunch, and dinner for a whole week.

The team took one last good look of the Sipi Falls from the balcony before leaving, and Will suggested us to visit the nearby attraction and learn about the history and geography of the region. He said that tourist guides should be available and he could accompany us for the entire duration of the tour.

Some cared less about this suggestion, but the rest of us, including myself, didn't want to go back so soon. Will drove all of us to a facility a few minutes away and stopped in front of a white low-rise building. This was the authentic visitor center.

A couple of courteous and well-dressed young men approached us and Will greeted them. A few moments later, one of them asked if we would like to walk around and he could brief us about Sipi Falls. Doctor Doug, Brenda, Shirley, June, and myself went along. Others, surprisingly the majority, preferred to stay in the van and waited.

Tourist guide #1 was reasonably professional yet quiet by nature. He took us to this "mini Sipi Falls"- the route that the official Sipi Falls flows through, for some pictures and explained to us the plants and flowers grown and flourished thanks to the naturally rich nourishment of the waterfall. Shirley was the happiest among all, to see the colorful and different kinds of flowers planted and blossomed.

The tourist guide stopped at a large shrub, pointed to us the unusually soft, palm-size green leaves, and asked us what we thought they were used for.

"For curing cuts and wounds, right?" June answered with a question, "Is that what mothers use as tissue paper on babies after they sneezed?

"Ugh, no."

"What is it?"

"This is a very common plant found in the rural parts of Uganda, and because of the size and delicate softness, children and adults alike use them for wiping."

"To wipe their faces?"

"No, after they went to the toilet."

I pretended to snatch a few pieces off and put them in my pouch, then told everyone that I may need bigger pieces after all.

I couldn't help but to contribute a fun wrap up for this rather boring scenic field trip.

Little did I realize, there was a hidden joker.

When the 7 of us, including Will and tourist guide #1, returned to the van, the rest of the team told us that tourist guide #2 had suggested to take them to a nearby cave for some exploration. The catch was, however, an "entrance fee" of 4,000 shillings per head (or 2 bucks). Because none of them had any local currency, that tourist guide gave up and disappeared.

"Is that a spot worth visiting though?" asked Doctor Doug, "if it was a once-in-a-lifetime-experience and they only charge us 2 dollars per person, then it was worth it."

"That shouldn't happen though," Will quickly responded, "this is an agency set up by the government to let foreign tourists explore Uganda's nature for free."

"Then don't bother," Shirley put in a strong opinion, "don't let them blackmail us, that's totally ridiculous."

Tourist guide #2 stood by the cave, visibly seen by all of us, appeared to be pissed by the impasse to make a few extra bucks and gave all of us a nasty look with his mouth wide open, yelling a local dialect.

Shirley shook her head and played charade with him, only without the yelling part.

It must have been flower power.

The tenseness in the van was soon relieved by a round of laughter of another unprecedented experience. Liz bought a live chicken and said that she wanted to cook us a fancy meal for the night. She will kill the chicken in her own kitchen right before cooking the dish. She threw the chicken into the back of the van and all the ladies were screaming and laughing as the chicken crowed and struggled to escape inside the back of the van.

That was so odd and hilarious, yet reportedly a popular practice among the locals.

I continued to sit at shotgun and just hoped that the craziness subsided once we return to the guesthouse. My throat started to hurt and I would request to see Doctor Doug before he returned to the clinic. I had another bad gut feeling.

****

"You have strap throat." Doctor Doug replied calmly.

"How did I get it?" I tried to pinpoint a specific incident where I might have either breathe in something extraordinarily smelly or drank some funny beverage.

"We wouldn't know," the doctor smiled pretentiously, "and it's pretty red too. Let me give you some pills and you'll be alright in a couple of days."

Great! Was it like the fourth time I got sick in 10 days?!

"So, doctor, how's the clinic going? I heard from Raeanne that you 2 got a lot done."

"It has been alright. We made use of almost every ounce of the equipment, medication, and supplies, and we collaborated with the doctors to get the kind of help they needed to treat the patients properly." Doctor Doug finished his statement in less than a second.

"May I stop by tomorrow for a visit? It's not like I know enough to help, but just to get to know more about the clinic and its conditions. I have been there once last week and didn't get to see much." I put on the most earnest face possible.

"Sure, anytime. But get some rest first."

I went back, took the pills, and napped for 2 hours. I woke up and became convinced that Doctor Doug did manage all the tasks at the clinic and took care of his patients effectively.

****

Liz kept her promise and served an exotic meal for dinner. The struggling chicken was deep fried and cut into several pieces with its innards attached. When I am healthy and hungry, I would have chewed on the flavorful chicken butt in no time, but the drowsy pills overpowered my appetite.

Three more days left- as I sat down quietly by myself and counted. Still weak as heck and didn't do much.

When could I get my big break, God? After returning to San Francisco?

Didn't feel like going back to bed right after dinner, I lingered in the dining room and observed the team's dynamics: John the retired stockbroker was quietly sitting by himself at a corner and spoke with the hosts and the ladies from time to time. At the other corner Bob, who had always been in endless conversations with Arlene and Doctor Doug whenever I saw him, continued to do so with a vigilant face. Shirley and June hung out as twins as usual. and Brenda, Allison, and Denise appeared to be getting along better and better.

Nothing has changed, and that left us with Pastor Mick, Raeanne, and myself as the random lone rangers.

Actually, if you include the hosts, that would have made 5. Liz was munching on the chicken wings and Will desperately wanted to talk with someone about anything. On better days, I would have gladly exchanged our opinions on basically whatever he wanted to talk about. Tonight, my fatigue had caused me to rudely ignore everyone.

I took out my Bible and searched for a scripture to lead the devotion I promised Pastor Mick in a couple of days. I was utterly clueless on how or where to begin.

A couple of doctors from the medical clinic came in and greeted our hosts. I looked up and caught a glimpse of a third guest. He looked like a doctor, but certainly not from the clinic.

Doctor Doug stepped up and shook hands with all 3 of them, apparently expecting their arrival.

I lowered my head and returned to my search, only to give up after a few minutes. How in the world was anyone supposed to find some verse in the Bible, create an interpretation, and ask the audience to relevantly apply the lesson learned?! I would have been delivering a sermon already if I could do that!

Being a perfectionist had always been painful.

Fine, fine, fine. Pastor Mick was sitting at the corner by himself, and I would not ask for his help. Let me do this the most unconventional way: I'll flip the pages of the Bible from the end and if I find a book that seemed interesting enough, I would stop, close my eyes, and randomly point to a chapter. Then, from that chapter I'll scientifically pick a verse that would best fit to what we have been experiencing in Uganda. If it's God's will for me to come to Africa and feel like a loser, then I won't doubt *His* selection for something as trivial as morning devotion.

I was exhausted. Anyway, here we go-

Blid, blid, blid, blid...

1, 2, 3, and stop!

That was a quick count. I flipped through the book of Revelation and stopped on the next book, the book of Jude, a very short and easily forgotten book when compared to the Gospel, Proverbs, or Genesis. It has one chapter comprised of 25 verses. *Phew!* That made it easy, I hoped.

Let me see now...hmm...alright, for the first 20 verses it talked about sinners, judgment, and punishment towards end time. What a *perfect* message for enlightenment and encouragement.

The last 20% of that chapter read like this though: "*Keep yourselves in the love of God, looking for the mercy of our Lord Jesus Christ unto eternal life. And of some have compassion making a difference; and others save with fear, pulling them out of the fire; hating even the garment spotted by the flesh. Now unto him that is able to keep you from falling, and to present you faultless before the presence of his glory with exceeding joy, to the only wise God our Savior, glory and majesty, dominion and power, both now and ever, Amen.*"

Decision made! I have something in mind to share that would complement this part of the book. It was just a matter of organizing them together, and to polish my pitiful public speaking skills.

Another sign from above had ascertained this pick. Within a fraction of a second a new friend pad on my shoulder and then onto the Bible.

"Aaaawwwwww!!!!!" I jumped out of my chair immediately and fling the holy book back and forth.

Clearly, the majority of the people in the room saw it coming and weren't surprised by my reaction. Pastor Mick approached and told me that the cockroach flew off already.

"No it hasn't!" I roared as I felt it tabbed and climbed on my upper back.

"Stopped! He's scared enough!" Shirley yelled at Pastor Mick as he jiggled.

I pretended to give him a nasty frown while guarding for the real thing to return.

"What?! C'mon man!" PM felt the threat.

"What's that thing there?" I pointed to his back with an innocent look.

"Ha ha, nice try; and it has teeth!" Pastor Mick smiled with his mouth opened wide, purposely showing his yellow teeth.

I needed to polish my acting skills too.

When this episode ended, Doctor Doug unfolded another one as he and Will returned from walking the 3 guests out. This time, it was a drama of a totally different nature.

"What's going on?" I asked Doctor Doug while he took his seat.

"Not much. Remember Sam?"

"Of course." How could I not?

"A doctor from Britain working in Mbale came to Dorcas and checked out on his eyes, and the news was that it was too late for any cure. When Sam was little, he had some minor eye diseases and his parents put some herbs on his eyes. His eyesight got worse and is likely that he will be totally blind soon."

"There is absolutely nothing that can be done?"

"Nope, and Sam's father knew about it. I don't know if Sam knows." Doctor Doug sighed.

Irony after irony seemed to be the name of the game in Uganda. The scariest part was that the locals have well adapted to this kind of livelihood. It was only foreigners like us that fret over misfortunate of others like a helpless baby.

"Hey Ambrose, I forgot to tell you something," Bob seized the chance as I was about to call it a day, "you remember Conrad? He came today and asked for you."

"Wow, that's amazing. What the heck did he want? What did you tell him?" I habitually put on a blank face whenever I suppressed my anger.

"I told him I don't know where you went. Then he left; but it looked like he will come back soon." Bob warned.

"Okay, thanks for the tip. Good night." I nodded with a weary smile, numbed.

The clock continued to tick, and I had to remain focused.

The drizzle hadn't stopped for a single day during this rainy season. The mud was still moist. The mosquitoes, and perhaps some cockroaches, were still buzzing around.

Ambrose Tse

Lord, I need your help. Give us the manifestation before it's too late.

Ambrose Tse

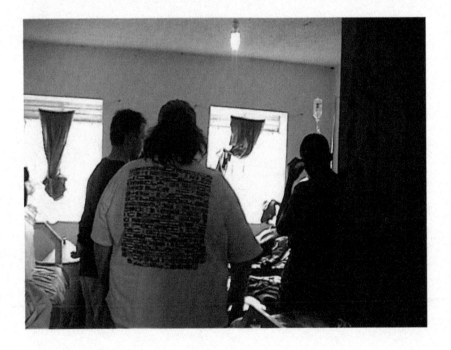

Chapter 11: Job Abandonment Violation

♪*Popeye the Sailorman boot boot!* ♫

That's the song that came to mind first thing in the morning after I opened my pair of gluey swollen eyes.

Hallelujah! No more sore throat. I felt like Popeye after eating a can of spinach. It's time to find and save Olivia!

Popeye would have to first fight Bluto before saving Miss Oyl. After I sat up on bed, Popeye turned into the famous fried chicken franchise boiling in my stomach. The virus had relocated to a more nutritious place overnight!

Fortuitously, Agne's popular tomato-omelet-in-a-waffle helped fight the diarrhea that I was determined to overcome, after spending 15 minutes flushing out the watery fertilizer. I snuck in an extra piece of that waffle before everyone showed up for breakfast, but missed the fun of finding out who didn't get his or her proper share.

The agenda for today was to lead worship at Dorcas just like what we did on the prior Saturday, except that it should be a shorter version. The children center expected to have less attendance from the outside on this Saturday.

For some reason, my enthusiasm died. It wasn't because of the diarrhea. It was something else. My zeal to participate in the worship team vanished as if I had better things to do.

But what? Pooping at the squatty-potty until the last juice drip out?

I cared about the kids. That's no doubt about it. I went to the gazebo for the quick rehearsal and headed out to Dorcas to reinvent the wheels.

Miraculously, whoever told us about having less audience redeemed the prediction, and the whole worship session could have been described as *perfect-* the music, the songs, the design, the flow, the spectators, and the leaders. Except that I wasn't mentally there.

Alright, alright, I gave up; it was the diarrhea. Time to rest like last time: I still have a few books written by Murakami Haruki that I would like to finish. I can then knock myself into a long coma until dinner time. I felt like I could just sleep for eternity and let Olivia be Bluto's girlfriend, or toothpick, as long as he pleased.

Murakami's short stories weren't as capturing as his lengthy novels, or some of his earlier works. Of course, a lot of his loyal fans may dispute that.

I was turning and tossing on the bed for hours. No coma and the diarrhea had subsided. The discomfort lingered as I sat up and waited for something to happen.

It wasn't until then I remembered the appointment I made with Doctor Doug at the clinic. I wondered if anyone would go with me, but nobody was available inside the guesthouse.

Fine, fine, fine. That could be even easier. I could stay for however long I wanted.

I quickly changed, grabbed my cameraman gears, and took my time to walk towards the little wooden structure.

"Hey, are you also going to the clinic?" Bob and Pastor Mick suddenly showed up from behind.

"Yes, and you two?"

"Oh, of course. Let's go in together." Will suddenly showed up behind Bob and Pastor Mick, and answered on their behalf.

That was creepy. The unexpected small gang uncannily gave me some confidence as I took a deep breath and marched towards another round of unknown.

A bit strange that neither Doctor Doug nor Raeanne was in the clinic. Will led the way into the backroom where all the in-house patients were staying at. A couple of local doctors and nurses were diagnosing a patient. I had no idea what to do, yet an invisible force was pushing me to step in just a little closer so that I won't miss anything.

Will, Bob, and one of the doctors stayed with me when we passed by the waiting room at the front to go into the patient room. Those few people sitting in the waiting room showed no reaction to our trespasses. According to that doctor, because of limited space there was no segregation between the different kinds of patients that were staying there. Indeed, the room was at most 100 square feet in area, and there was about half a foot of space between each bed. Pregnant moms, children with a broken limb, and men with skin diseases can be found all in the same ward, and they were all motionless.

That was an expected scenario, I thought. But I suddenly sensed that something unusual was going on.

It was too quiet.

It sounded like nobody was in the room. It felt like nothing was going on. Why? Shouldn't there be some mourning, wailing, baby crying, or at least people talking?

Still, not much has changed since the last time the whole team took a brief tour on the first day of our arrival.

I felt a chill rapidly conquering the upper back. How I wished I had better prepared for the very next scene.

177

Don't be mistaken though: there was no gross imageries like an amputated arm dangling from a guy's shoulder, or blood pouring out from the eyes, ears, and nostrils of anyone. In fact, the room was even smaller than I anticipated, hosting less than a dozen patients, and the atmosphere was mellow. Will and the doctor were leading Bob, Pastor Mick, and me to the bedside of this one particular little boy in the middle of the room.

The doctor told us that this boy was recently picked up from the street by Liz, and not much was known about his physical condition or identity, other than the apparent fact that he had malnutrition and tuberculosis. It was not clear either if he would be able to make it for more than a few days.

I was staring at him but couldn't see him very clearly. All I could tell was that his eyes were disproportionally humungous and even more watery than mine. The peeling skin wrapped tightly around his rib cage and he didn't look like he had a stomach. I meant, the concave curve was so bend that even the intestines appeared to be missing. He was beyond emaciated. More than half a dozen of flies and mosquitoes were loitering nearby, and some rested on the boy's cheeks and eyes, as if an all-you-can-eat buffet was about to be served. I took a deep breath and turned at the rest of the gang.

"You are welcome to take a picture if you want to." Will thought he knew what our next question would be.

What?! Why did he say that? Was it because he became so numb already that from his perspective it would be more beneficial for the community to have us take a picture of a dying kid, show it to the world, so that more people would cast their concerns to the conditions here in Africa? If someone were to put her- / himself in the boy's shoes, how would s/he feel when some stranger takes a picture of her / him when s/he is in such a gravely condition?

Or, Will must have overrated our emotional strengths.

I was literally frozen for 10 seconds, debating if I should even take my camcorder out.

Ka-chark!

Suddenly, a bright flesh that whitened the whole ward attacked from behind. I turned around and saw Bob took out his camera to finish my job proficiently. I was in utter shock. In a fraction of a second, a story that I've heard in a sermon from more than 3 years ago in a conference resurfaced:

"One day, a BBC (British Broadcasting Company) reporter named Malcolm Breckenridge interviewed Mother Theresa about her ministry in Calcutta, India, where she started a hospice called the 'Home for the Dying'. Each day, she would go to the streets and pick up some sick, dying homeless folks and bring them back to this center to wash them up and send them on their way. She has been doing this for years and the reporter asked her: 'What's the point of doing all this? Does it solve the problems of India?' Mother Theresa answered: 'I don't believe there is a collective solution to a problem. I believe in a person-to-person solution. *Since there is only one Jesus, that's the person I need to help at that moment.*"

The main theme of that conference was about faith in the middle of turbulent times, delivered after a regional financial crisis and right before the turn of the millennium.

After making sure that the camera bag zipper was closed all the way, I went up by the side of the bed and prayed for the boy quietly. He looked so fragile that I didn't even dare to place my hand on him. "*Father God, you know him better than all of us here. If it is your will to take him, I ask that you will end his pain sooner than later, and that you will accept him into your heavenly kingdom. If not, please cure him and give him the hope of life and to know you*".

Popeye's spinach was this prayer.

The short prayer could have been done better without the stuttering. We didn't really do anything else but took off shortly after that. To fulfill my role as the team's cameraman, I took a picture of Pastor Mick stretching his hand out and prayed audibly for every other patient from behind. The boy, whom we called Joseph, reportedly hung on until the last day we were in Uganda.

I could only wish that the latter part of my short prayer became a reality.

In retrospect, it made sense that it was so quiet in the room. None of the patients would have enough energy to mourn or cry.

On the way back, I was walking behind Bob and debated if I should ask him about his rationale for taking that picture. Before I spoke, he stopped walking, turned his head around, and looked at me.

"That was sad, huh?" I asked.

"Yeah, I was overwhelmed."

"Sometimes I ask God why things like this happen for no good reason."

"I am confused too." Bob looked shaken.

"Well, as least they have nothing else to compare with. To them, life is how they are currently living in." I tried to distract and sound philosophical.

"That's true." Bob nodded and ended the dialogue singlehandedly as he disappeared behind the door once we have returned to the guesthouse.

I will definitely find a better time and try to ask him again.

To his credit, Bob took at least a hundred more pictures than I did. From the pictures he sent to everyone in the group after the trip, it appeared that he pressed the shutter button almost every other minute while he was awake.

What's next? I stood there and asked myself.

Pastor Mick wasn't around. He probably stuck around at the clinic to ask the doctors more questions and spend more time in prayer. I couldn't even catch a glimpse of Doctor Doug or Raeanne's shadow anywhere.

Geez, thanks Jesus for all the "gut feeling" that led me to realize how impotent I was.

I looked up into the sky. It was covered with clouds as if it were about to pour like cats and dogs. It hasn't fulfilled its daily routine yet.

"I will lift up mine eyes unto the hills, from whence cometh my help. My help cometh from the LORD, which made the heaven and earth." Psalms 121: 1-2.

Subsequently, I found this scripture in the Bible and took comfort in. How I wished I could have read the Bible more often and kept the words in my heart more vigilantly.

****

The beautiful sunset had drawn all the birds back to their nests. For the team, a meeting was scheduled to be held to decide who will do what after the trip.

At exactly 6pm, everyone gathered around a circle in the dining room and Arlene started the announcement: "I am sure everyone is aware that we only have two more days to spend at Dorcas and the clinic, and I hope that everyone is having a good time. As our time here approaches to an end, there is a few things that we wanted to make sure they get done after we return to the U.S., therefore…"

Blah, blah, blah. Thanks for reminding us your supreme leadership. I couldn't help to be sarcastic without rolling my eyes.

Similar to the meeting held at the FCA center in Modesto a couple of months ago, my mind wandered off after I *shockingly* realized that my job as the assistant treasurer and the cameraman was to turn in the books and records and disseminate the pictures shortly after the trip was over.

Towards the end of the meeting, however, a concern (or gossip, however you want to interpret that) raised by Shirley captured everyone's attention: "You guys know what happened this morning? I overheard two Africans that were standing right outside of the orphanage conspiring ways to get money from those "rich Americans". They said that since we will be leaving soon, they will need to do it fast." Shirley was as pissed off as usual, and finally exclaimed: "What's wrong with these people?!"

Nobody answered her question directly, but one of the ladies added: "You guys should also be careful with Jacqueline, the nurse with a vocal gift at the clinic. She always asks for stuff from clothes and toiletries to basically anything you have."

Arlene looked at everyone's face, paused, and warned: "Just be careful with strangers and those you have just met other than Will and Liz, okay?"

A logical question to ask Shirley was the language those locals spoke in, but no one wanted to play the devil's advocate. I was so glad that I did not look like a rich American. Or even an American, most of the time. Conrad did however get through me, thanks to my inexperience, faulty assumptions, and inflexibility. Yet no one else approached me for any other sketchy offers afterwards.

While everyone put the chairs back after the meeting was adjourned, Arlene asked me: "Do you have a few minutes Ambrose?"

"Sure. How can I help you?" I put on the most sincere face ever.

"We actually started this yesterday and hopefully we can finish it today: you know that at FCA our primary job is to help those in the U.S. who would like to adopt or sponsor children from other countries, and given that we are already here, we thought we should create some profiles for those in the neighborhood that are in need. Or, conversely, to give the adopters more choices to choose from. Since you are the team's cameraman, I would like to see if you can give us a hand and take a picture of each of the kids." Arlene put on an even more sincere face and delivered her message in a soft tone.

Oh, it was a side favor. Fine for a good cause.

"You want me to just take a nice picture for each of these kids and send them to you afterwards?"

"Yup."

"Okay. I can use my camcorder but I must tell you in advance that the quality may not be as good as a regular digital camera." I put forth a disclaimer.

"That's alright." Arlene smiled.

A dozen kids had already lined up outside of the dining room during our conversation. Pastor Mick, John, and Bob helped organize them.

A couple of boys stepped in and both looked clueless. Liz, our interpreter, spoke with them and they looked relieved.

Ambrose Tse

Arlene couldn't be happier and asked me to take a picture with her wrapping the two boys around her arms, one on each side. One of them looked equally as happy, while the other annoyed. It was a pretty funny scene.

The more cheerful kid got to take the picture first. He appeared so happy and proud that he took out a piece of candy and started munching it as I pressed the shutter button. Arlene and Liz told him to put that away immediately.

He looked pissed for the second picture, but I didn't tell Arlene about that. It was too funny.

The funny moments ended quickly after the more serious boy got his turn. Something was seriously wrong with these pictures.

It was not only because John refused to move out of the background, but more importantly the pixels were so big that the pictures were obviously of low quality.

That's what happened when you use a camcorder to take pictures.

"Hey Arlene, you know what, the pictures are pretty blurry. I am not sure if I can fix them." I gave her my honest opinion.

Arlene didn't respond, but Bob did: "That's fine. I have my camera with me and it has enough room for a few hundred more."

Without verifying my pictures, Bob took over in a smooth, natural transition.

I have had enough. I took a deep breath, turned around, and headed back to the bedroom until dinner time.

Ten minutes later, I came back to the room for dinner.

Food was the best tool for reconciliation in a group setting ever. Period.

Agnes served 2 comforting meals on the same day: after having the tomato-omelet-in-a-waffle for breakfast, we now have a boiled tilapia cut into cross sections and boiled in a brown savory broth, along with a large bowl of perfectly baked mashed potatoes topped with slices of peppers and carrots for dinner. I gave myself a few scoops of the crusty mashed potatoes on the top, and picked up the large pieces of lean tilapia meat attached to the bone. Other people can enjoy the skins and flakes. I didn't care about etiquette anymore.

My weak digestion was forcing me to focus instead on Joseph's condition and process the experience. Little did I know, there was more to come.

Ambrose Tse

Chapter 12: Joining the Acrobat Team

"Are we there yet?"

About an hour later, I whispered to the driver the most intelligent question in the world like a little kid. The driver either didn't hear me or simply ignored me.

The van continued to speed on the bumpy muddy road. I rolled down the window and took several pictures of the scenery on the roadside.

****

Liz decided to bring the team to a fancier church close to Mbale for us to experience different kinds of Ugandan worship. Nobody objected since she also emphasized that she would need to go to the marketplace in Mbale to buy some groceries and make us some nice dinner before we return home.

It was a long ride, and no one got the hints when the driver pulled over at a gas station 5 minutes after we hit the road. Most of us were sidetracked by how others bought gas for "take out".

"Look at that! Isn't it amazing?!" I pointed to the side and turned around from the shotgun seat, hoping that someone saw what I saw.

A man carrying a small empty plastic bag walked up to an attendant next to a pump, and they spoke softly and briefly about something. Then, he opened and yanked the month of that bag with both hands to let the attendant place the nozzle right on top and fill his share.

Not one single drip was spilled, and the man casually spun the bag, tied a knot, and returned to his parked bike with one hand on the handle bar and drove off.

187

"Wow, this guy better be careful! I can't believe he is taking such risk carrying the bag just like that!" I couldn't help but raised my concern.

No one responded.

I cared less. All I wanted was to get our driver moving again as soon as he finished filling up!

Fortunately, we didn't see that man again, and no catastrophe occurred.

From the paved main road to the smaller mud-covered alleys, the driver never hesitated to slow down as if car maintenance wouldn't cost him anything. A headache evolved so I gave up on the photo shoot and rolled the window back up.

Liz was absolutely right about the fancier surrounding of this church. The premise was a lot bigger, greener, and more comfortable. A playground with swings, basketball poles, and a soccer field was constructed in front of it. Similar to the first church we went to, a school was built adjacent to the sanctuary. On the side of one wall, a "list" of school objectives was painted:

1. TO IMPROVE ON HYGIENE AND SANITATION FACILITIES.
2. TO PROVIDE MIDDAY MEALS AT SCHOOL FOR ALL PUPILS.
3. TO PROVIDE MORE MATERIALS FOR PHYSICAL FITNESS.
4. TO ENCOURAGE PUPILS TO MAKE SITING FACILITIES THROUGH ART S CRAFT.
5. TO PRODUCE GARDEN MANAGEMENT SKILLS THROUGH AGRICULTURE.
6. TO PROVIDE FIRST AID FACILITIES.

Not sure why the extra spacing for #6. I took comfort in the fact that the students, or pupils, were given some kind of directions to sustain themselves.

Thanks to the driver's reckless driving, we made it to the service just before the crowd rushed in. We later found out that it actually didn't really matter, because a special time has been designated for us, the special guests from the U.S., during service.

My only hope was to sing praises and worship God like the rest of the congregation, regardless of the language barrier.

But of course, a team has to cooperate and function together as a team. When we took our seats as a group in the front, a dozen choir members, all clothed in royal dark purple robes, simultaneously took their positions for some eye-opening actions.

My first live gospel music performance was a blast!

All 12 singers, all of them large women (large in terms of lung capacity), began to clap their hands to an energetic beat and swung their bodies from left to right with their arms flung to the front. Their vigor wiped away my headache when they moved within inches from where I was sitting. Timidity was definitely a taboo during this sacred praise time. The in-your-face sentiment could very well qualify for a wild rock concert!

Too bad filming wasn't allowed inside the sanctuary.

The best part took place towards the end of this 20-minute non-stop presentation. As soon as the drum and music stopped, one by one the choir members stepped forward and sang a solo part with assurance and power.

What they were singing had to be praises. Even if language were a barrier, the tone could not have been a melancholic one or anything otherwise.

Each of them took about half a minute and systematically stepped back to let the next singer step up and did her solo. At the end, the choir wrapped up with another commanding song that literally shook the fat around Pastor Mick's and my belly.

Hmm… language barrier…what else could I say about this?

Not much. The preacher took over the podium and delivered a sermon in an authoritative tone in Kiswahili (another assumption) for the next 20 minutes. The congregation, including our team, kept our heads down and remained motionless until he finished.

The speaker stepped down, and there was a moment in transition when the stage was completely empty.

A choir member, along with Liz, held Arlene's hand, with one of the ministers on her other side, slowly walked up and made an announcement, presumably in Kiswahili again.

That was apparently an unexpected move for the most of us. Everyone but a few in the team looked at each other cluelessly and waited for further development.

Someone handed Liz a big, beautiful, traditional white Ugandan dress for her to give to Arlene after making a short speech.

"They must be honoring Arlene for all she has done from before and this trip." One of the ladies stated the obvious.

Few other older local ladies wearing a similar dress went up and help Arlene to put the new, bulky dress on. At the end, they put a thick, blue cloth around her waist and tied a knot in the front.

Arlene couldn't be happier.

I was hoping that someone would fill me in on what exactly Arlene or FCA had done, but nobody seemed to have an answer.

Fortunately, the service didn't just end there.

Unlike the previous Sunday, there was a time for tithe and offering, and this church had adopted the universal routine of passing the baskets row by row until the ushers recollected them at the back of the sanctuary.

This gave me a headache. I had in my pocket only a handful of shillings that I intended to spend on souvenirs towards the end of this trip and for emergency only, and I wasn't sure if I had enough or will have to go to a bank for exchanges again for the team. Should I ignore the basket and look the other way? Or should I see what everyone else had decided?

What should I do? I did want to give something very practical to this church.

Wait- I had most of the shillings, and John had the rest since he was the appointed official treasurer. None of the other teammates could donate unless they put in US dollars.

Ah ha! US dollars might be a good option!

But what would the church do with some foreign currency?

I had to make my decision quickly as the plate was fast approaching,

I took my wallet out and searched for something that could be used, and found a wrinkly 10-dollar bill.

That should do it. It was better than nothing, right? The locals would find a way to exchange it into shillings, somehow. Oh heck, even Conrad was willing to take US dollars in small denominations for his scam!

I threw in my offering without delay and swiftly put the rest of the blink-blink back into hiding.

My fellow comrades did not put in anything into the basket. After all, they were guests, right?

When the baskets finally reunited with the ushers in the front, I took a curious peak and noted the pitiful accumulations.

The quiet crowd suddenly turned lively when the tithe and offering portion of the service came to an end. Chatters were flying from all corners and some people got up from their seats.

"Is the service already over?" I twisted my neck from left to right and back and forth, and turned around and noted that nobody was leaving though.

"!Noostiteg?revetahwforiapecinsihtstnawohw!emitnoitcuas'ti!"

A local man took his time and walked up to the stage with two baskets full of "something" from the back and started to talk really fast and energetically, pointing his fingers to both sides of the crowd. Most of the audience gave their attention, while only a few of them raised their hands and responded.

"Dlos!" After a few rounds of interaction, the short, assertive phase was always the standard happy ending.

The auction was obviously a success, and my jaw dropped to the ground to have learned that it was part of the tradition!

"C'mon buddy, surprise me with more of the indigenous stuff!" I almost yelled out loud.

Once again they did.

The service had finally come to an end, when a minister seriously took the podium and made a relatively lengthy and less authoritative speech. My teammates and I guessed that it was most likely announcement time.

After what-seemed-to-be-the-last-piece-of-news was made, suddenly everyone, and I meant literally *everyone,* in the congregation frantically cheered and applauded as if they have won the lottery.

No riot, and no doubt that the outburst was a cheerful hooray.

"What happened?" I posted another open question in the air.

This time, unexpectedly, Doctor Doug was the one who caught my query: "I think they are cheering for something we gave them as gifts." He turned to the other side and asked Will for the specifics. "Oh, we gave them a couple of soccer balls and a pump."

"Oh, I see. But no frisbees?" I asked with a sarcasm tone in an innocuous mode.

Doctor Doug honestly shook his head: "I doubted it."

Of course, nobody would have noticed or remember something so trivial related to frisbees.

But I did. I was a professional auditor with good memory.

Before my conceitedness inflated and reflected on my chubby face, another twist captured the everyone's attention, and I again meant *everyone* in the congregation. The ushers took the offerings out from the baskets and screamed a set of coarse phrases. They kept searching for more tithe inside the baskets.

Those sitting nearby helped them look for more potentially missing blink-blink dropped somewhere on the ground.

It couldn't be my offering…could it? It was only 10 bucks. Or were they surprised to find a U.S. bill?

On second thought, if I would have remembered that a minister in Uganda reportedly made only $40 a month and done the math correctly, Mr. George Washington would have sufficed.

Gosh, how I hated to have created such unnecessary stir.

The ushers' vision slowly shifted across the hall onto the team with an excited facial expression. I hastily jogged my way through the crowd and left the sanctuary as quickly as possible when the congregation was dismissed after doxology. Keeping a low profile in a foreign land was a survival skill proven to work, especially after the ordeal with Conrad.

Call me paranoid, but at least nobody followed me despite my highly noticeable face. It was fortunate that I never looked like a rich American.

After the majority of the attendees exited the building, the team sort of lounged around at the outside and waited for further directions from either Will or Liz, who were still inside with Arlene and talking with various other locals. Meanwhile, Bob was checking on his camera, so I walked towards him.

"Hey! When did you bring the balls over?" Another intelligent question; but my elation was at its peak ever since arriving at Uganda.

"Oh, we have a few extra ones after giving the soccer balls to Dorcas, so Will and Liz suggested to donate a couple of them to this church." Bob was still busy checking his camera.

"I am sure they will love them."

"I hope so." Bob finally looked up and mysteriously looked a little stern after saying so.

Bob and I kept walking downhill and continued our small talk. A flock of boys, teenagers, young adults, and old men all stormed towards the large piece of flatland where a skinny cow was leisurely lying.

Part!

A neon yellowish green soccer flied right over our heads and rolled into the combat zone. Over two dozen guys of all ages joined in to check out the new toy.

If anyone believed that the way these grown-ups played this game would be any different than the children at Dorcas, think again. Regardless of who, when, and where, the *how* remained the same: each player would chase after the ball no matter what position he was playing, kept kicking the ball to somewhere once his foot touches it, and shoot it wherever there was a slight chance of touching the goal pole. Passing the ball was a rare instance.

It was all for fun, right? Wrong!

This official national sport provided more than mere entertainment. It symbolized as opportunities for those gifted ones to practice and eventually become a world class player to escape out of poverty.

The funniest part of the scene though had to be the stationary cow. It was sleeping in the middle of the unofficial soccer field and no one dare to disturb it. Or, rather, the cow cared less about the ongoing chaotic action.

It was nonetheless encouraging to see them play soccer.

195

A man wearing a suit was battling to steal the ball away from a shirtless kid, who stubbornly retained possession and passed by his opponent with a fake, nimble move.

Wow, that was cool!

More team members joined and became speechless spectators. One of the ladies walked up to us and said: "The pastor and his family are inviting us to stay for lunch at his home. It's right next to the church. So come along."

"Have fun guys!" I whispered inaudibly and waved at them, who were too busy to respond.

The timing for a meal couldn't be better. Climbing back up on the hill was a pain in the butt. Fortunately, the pastor's hut was literally adjacent to the church as told.

This was the first time I stepped into the interior of a residential hut, even though many pictures had been taken on the outside.

Thanks to the natural light that funneled through the back window, it became clear that the set up of a hut was almost exactly like that of an icehouse (per National Graphics). There was a large common area used for dining, family gathering, bedroom, etc. The bunk beds were concealed by a large piece of cloth for privacy purposes, just like the ones in Dorcas' boys dorm rooms.

Several pieces of twisted cloth attached to the wooden structure supporting the tin roof were tied in a series and hung vertically from the top. They were decorated with some green and blue ribbons usually seen only during Christmas time.

A piece of paper was taped in the middle of one of the cloth-tile, and it read:

"MY HOUSE IS PROTECTED BY THE BLOOD OF JESUS CHRIST"

Confession: I almost wanted to steal that sign and hang it in my own bedroom.

The pastor's family was extremely hospitable, without being excessively overt about their sentiment. You could tell so by the number and amount of different local dishes they placed on top of the short table. The 12 of us, plus Will and Liz, sat around the table and the hosts quietly passed the plates, utensils, and food around. The traditional Ugandan dishes like millets, matoke, chopped spinach, and beans were served. The matoke was wrapped around by a large piece of banana leaf that shaped like a giant tortoise, and the portion was large enough to feed more than 20 famish farmers. Remembering a time when I ate lots of pasta for lunch on a weekday and became full and drowsy for the rest of the afternoon, I only took a spoonful of the stuffy empty carbs. With all due respect, I smiled and rubbed my belly to the pastor's wife that I had enough for my "small" appetite.

A good old half an hour of tranquil lunch spent with the indigenous folks.

It was really getting late. We thanked our host for the meal and took off for Mbale.

Shockingly, the soccer game had finally ended, and all the guys disappeared to nowhere. The more fascinating transition took place while we were eating: it was now the ladies' turn to play.

A volleyball game was set up nearby using the same neon yellowish green soccer ball, and the girls were laughing so hard as if they had won first place in a beauty pageant contest.

The second soccer ball became the target of a mini 3-on-3 co-ed basketball game. A "basketball game" was just a label I subconsciously put on, because there was no backboard at each of

197

the hoops on either end. The added difficulty didn't hinder the laughter.

Next time when I come to Africa again, I swear that I will bring a variety of balls, and I will insist on no frisbee, even if the bags were fully packed.

Wait- a couple of guys from afar were throwing a plastic disk. I thought Doctor Doug said he "doubted it"?!

Well, he wasn't the person I should have asked in the first place.

The two men were tossing the new toy like the boys at Dorcas, and appeared to be enjoying the game more because of better control and gripping techniques.

Alright, alright, I will reverse my decision.

At any rate, God, thanks for the electrifying redemption.

****

The ride to Mbale was relatively shorter than the one in the morning. But because of some light drizzle the road got really muddy and sticky, the driver could not race as fast as he did earlier. About 30 minutes later, Will's car and the van parked on the side of a main road, and Liz got off to buy grocery for dinner. She said she will be back shortly.

Mbale... the marketplace was as crowded and noisy as the last time we were here.

While we all sat in the van with the door slid open for ventilation, Doctor Doug took out his camcorder and checked on it. An old lady with a hunchback walked by and took note of

Doctor Doug's gadget, and stood in front of him to observe what he was doing.

I was so worry for Doctor Doug. At the same time, I was confused about his lack of vigilance and inaction to the stranger's stare. The lady acted like as if the camcorder was hers and Doctor Doug was the repairman. They were physically *that* close.

My anxiety was not without reason thanks to the haunting riot. The old lady's curiosity could potentially draw more people and unnecessarily popularized the team. As far as the rest of the team was concerned, no one else seemed to care about the uninvited visitor.

Doctor Doug remained super calm. He was totally unaffected by the unsolicited stare. When he finally acknowledged the lady's presence, he looked up and asked the lady: "Wasn't it fun to play with this little machine?"

The old lady smiled. I couldn't tell if she understood the doctor's question. Technology has always been a magnet for people of all ages.

The lady hadn't given up yet, not until Doctor Doug finally fixed whatever the problem was and put the camcorder away. Then, she uttered a few words softly and walked away with a smile.

What a strange incident.

What was more strange was Liz's definition of "shortly". Half an hour later, we couldn't even catch her shadow.

"You know what," Arlene came out of Will's car to the van, "there is something that we need to buy for the workers at Dorcas and the clinic. When Liz comes back, let her know that we will be back as soon as we finished shopping." John, Will, and Bob, joined her for their business.

Great! Our ride home would take even longer. Please, delay no more!

Coincidentally, Liz came back with bags of grocery *shortly* after those four left. After one of us told her what happened, she looked a little surprised and said "Okay, let's spend a few more moments here. I will wait here until everyone comes back. But be quick though, be back by 4pm since it will take almost an hour to go back, and the Dorcas kids have prepared a drama to show us. And Agnes will need some time to cook."

Good! At least there were some directions. I looked at my watch when I stepped out of the van, and noted that there was still 20 minutes left.

Feeling the vibe of Mbale's marketplace for one last time was surely a privilege, especially when you could get around by yourself after retrieving a mental map from short-term memory. People were packed in the alleys and on the streets during this sunny Sunday afternoon, possibly because of the light drizzle from an hour ago.

Slipping through the crowd alone gave me a strange sense of comfort, which then gave me the idea to search for four-member gang that told the team to wait in the van.

It was easier than I thought.

Once I made a left turn in the middle of an alley and another right into a hidden, smaller marketplace, John was standing in front of a shoe booth, observing the different kinds of supplies available for sale.

I greeted him and asked what he was doing.

"The staff at Dorcas and the nearby church needed some plastic boots on rainy days. You know, all they have are sandals, if not walking barefooted. And it's always muddy everywhere." John reassured me slowly.

I glanced over at the six pairs of boots they bought. They were the heavy-duty kind that people wear when they do serious gardening or landscaping work in a forest. And they costed like a few bucks for a pair.

Other booths in this secluded marketplace area included a barber shop, a wig shop, a store selling bamboo and ropes, a hardware store that also sold household items like backpacks, batteries, and umbrellas, a woman clothing store, and a mattress shop.

It was almost four o'clock. I told John what Liz said about the drama at Dorcas, and everyone hurried back to the van.

The sky was getting cloudier and darker.

****

"Is the closing ceremony still on?" I looked up the gloomy sky and doubted.

"As far as I know." answered one of the ladies.

It had been a long day traveling for everyone. The kids at Dorcas were reportedly more zealous than ever to perform for us.

Liz dropped the grocery off for Agnes and after the team took a short potty break, we headed back out to the familiar place.

The weather had once again fulfilled its daily routine in a timely manner. This time though, it poured pretty harsh and went on for a couple of hours. But thank God, the large rain drops didn't fall until everyone arrived at Dorcas.

It was dark, however; not pitch black but it was the kind of annoying dark that forced you to decide if you should turn the lights on and drop the shades or not. It was the time of the day that prompted you to simply stop any ongoing activities and just sit back, relax, and enjoy a drink. Or so-call "happy hour" in some places.

What made it even more difficult to focus was the lack of street light, or anything that beamed. There were no cars, buildings, flashlights, or anything that could have helped. The sound the children made however led the way, and would not permit anyone to get lost.

"This play is about the celebration of a sick person who was healed because of the power from Jesus." Someone made that announcement before the skit started.

The Children Center was packed with other small audiences waiting to also see the show. The heavy rain forced the crowd to scatter to different areas with a covering, such as the classroom behind the stage or right in front of the boy's dorm on the side.

I looked around but couldn't find either mini Beyonce or Alan. Maybe… that was it? No last final goodbye? Well, I shouldn't be expecting too much to begin with.

The 3 and only 3 perfectly normal chairs were placed in the middle of the stage, while a dozen of the older kids lined up behind the chairs and started to prepare for their usual vivacious dance and drum beating as a prelude.

Here's a problem: Liz directed all of us, the honorable guests, to sit in the "VIP" row at the front and enjoy the performance, but there were only 9 chairs.

I hesitated and pondered on what to do next. Arlene, Shirley, John, etc. comfortably claimed their thrones in the middle and suited themselves to some of the shaky ones.

Fine, fine, fine, my butt was too big for any of the empty seats anyway.

An open spot was available a few feet away from the stage, right at the front of the boy's dorm. I quickly squeezed myself in while making a silly face to the young bystanders and occupied that space, only to be surrounded by about 10 children almost immediately.

Mingling and standing with everyone else in the crowd was probably the least I could do.

Da da da, da da da, da da da...

The noise made by the rain drops when they hit the slanted rusty tin roof was loud and rhythmical, but it didn't interfere the viewership of the performance.

The songs the singers began presenting were in the local dialect, and the crowd behind the VIPs were stretching their necks to get a better grasp of what they were about. All others who were standing elsewhere were also paying serious attention to the development of the singing, and later the skit.

After a round of chanting, laughter, body twisting, and spinning that lasted 10 minutes, the 3 normal chairs on the stage were pushed up against the wall, and a foam mattress was placed in the middle. A girl lied down on that mattress, pretended to be sick, and a narrator stepped in and commenced an introduction.

I was guessing that the actors and actresses were reenacting one of the bible stories where a sick widow, in faith, approached Jesus and asked for healing. The whole village celebrated her recovery and turned their convictions to Christ. It was one of the more straightforward stories recorded in the gospel that were taught quite frequently during Sunday school.

The weather had not been kind to the hardworking performers. The heavy rain showed no sign of stopping and the mushy mud kept accumulating everywhere.

Some of the five- and six-year-olds that stood around me appeared to have gotten lost of the skit and grew impatient. The rain however kept them from doing anything else. I started to give out hi-fives to keep them somewhat entertained.

"What the?!"

Just when I turned to my right and tried to disturb a cute little girl, suddenly she took out a blue plastic cup from nowhere, stretched her arm out, filled the cup with the rain water dripping down the roof, and took a long sip out of that cup for her happy hour special.

Too late- she finished her beverage way before I could react. She looked extremely satisfied with the natural thirst quencher.

Other kids didn't have a cup, so several of them followed her by opening their mouths wide, stuck their tongues out, and let the rainwater flow in directly and slowly.

All of them did this exceptionally quietly to give the performers their proper respect.

My eyes remained wide open, recalling the rusty rooftops that I saw in pictures of the panoramic views of the cities in some developing countries.

I continued to look at the direction of where the stage was, and put forth a silent, civilized prayer:

"God, I give up. I thank you for this opportunity to fly me all the way out here to Uganda and found out what life was really like in a rural area. But I couldn't handle the fact that there were so much unfulfilled basic needs within the local communities, and there was absolutely NOTHING that a lay person like me could do for these innocent ones that needed the most help and care. Wait, let me go back. The soccer balls did help a bit. At any rate, I am even getting sick and tired of complaining all this to you. You knew exactly what I was going to say even before I opened my mouth..."

The short, internalized "outburst" was cut short by a round of warm applause when the play was finally over before I realized it. The singers also returned to the stage for a humble bow. Liz and one of the instructors of Dorcas who orchestrated the performance went up and prayed for everyone. Finally, Liz thanked the instructor and briefly encouraged the youngster before they were let go.

The rain had also miraculously stopped, moments before we were about to return to the guesthouse for dinner.

It was a few minutes before 7pm according to my watch. The event took less than two hours, but it felt so, so, so long already.

The hydrated little girl, along with her friends, scattered without a trace.

****

The muddy unpaved roads soaked up a large portion of the precipitation into the soil, thanks to the massive downpour, which also created fewer puddles. The unexpected inconvenience was that it took twice as much time and energy to walk on these grounds.

A 5-minute commute from Dorcas back to the guesthouse now took more than 10 minutes. Each and everyone on the team made the extra effort to lift their legs up high and moved forward, leaving behind some unusually large and deep footprints.

Will, Liz, and other pedestrians passed by and gave us the unintentional stare.

"Take your time, okay?" Will smiled, "We will go back to the guesthouse first."

I was almost absolutely positive that Will wasn't making fun of his VIP guests.

The nice dinner Liz promised to serve was surely a fantastic one, at least to me personally. You guessed it: the main dish was a whole roasted young goat!

I had no idea where the goat came from, or how Agnes and others managed to cook this baby in such a short period of time. This "baby" certainly wasn't a baby, it was large enough to feed over 20 adults. Liz invited a few of the staff from the clinic to enjoy the meal together, to celebrate a friend who finally graduated from medical school, and to say farewell to us just in case we won't see each other again.

Most of the team, again, stayed away from the gamey stuff.

Roger, Sidney, and Godfrey all came with the fresh grad and brought a small fancy cake to share.

"So, who's taking care of the clinic right now?" I pretended to play hardball with Godfrey, the most innocuous looking doctor of all.

"We have a nurse staying there now, and she knows we are here if she needs us. We'll go back to the clinic after the party's over." Godfrey replied softly.

I pushed a little further: "I am just playing with you! Of course I trust that there is someone over there right now. But I am just wondering about this boy that we saw yesterday. We didn't get his name but he had some serious malnutrition and tuberculosis. How is he doing now? Do you know who I am talking about?"

Godfrey looked at me in the eye and spent a few moments to search for the answer: "I think you are talking about Joseph. We gave him some medicine and he is in stable conditions now."

"That's good to know." I was betting that we were talking about the same person, and Godfrey spoke with professional integrity.

Feeling sorry for being a little too demanding, Godfrey and I made some small talks about our trip and life in San Francisco. Godfrey then turned the table around and asked me a very interesting question: "So, what are the top spiritual strongholds from where you came from?"

Caught totally unprepared, I hesitated and replied with a smile: "Well, there are a lot. From my point of view, in general it would be consumerism and just plain old disobedience when people still went ahead and do what they weren't supposed to do. You know, America is a free country, and it's hard to tell people what to do and what not to do."

"Hmm...I see." Godfrey fell into deep thoughts but responded: "I'll pray for you and your country."

BAM!

If it was just some dude from church that said the same thing, I would have taken it with a grain of salt. But Godfrey's passion and serious expression told me that no one should discount what he said.

And he brought up a good point; something really simple and helpful: pray.

He knew that there wasn't much he could do about the strongholds I casually mentioned, but he cared and prayed.

That turned me into a series of deep thoughts before I went to bed later.

"And the spiritual strongholds of Uganda? Can you tell me what you think they are?"

"I would say alcoholism, witchcraft, and other faiths." Godfrey sounded like he knew exactly I would ask the same question in return.

"Oh yeah, that's right, Uganda brews its own beer. And I've heard that they are pretty good." I obnoxiously suggested.

"They are," Godfrey smiled, "but people get drunk and they cause trouble. It's definitely a bad thing."

"Oh of course, and I will also pray for Uganda about these." I needed to show that I genuinely cared too.

We grinned at each other comfortably, knowing that they weren't just fluff.

****

With all the dialogues going on, it looked like dinner would go well passed 10pm. If the power were to be cut off by that time as usual, then I would have no other time to prep for my turn to lead morning devotion the very next day. I didn't forget the promise made to Pastor Mick, and for the past few days I have been worrying about what to say and how to convey the message from the book of Jude. Judging from what my other teammates had shared, it sounded like you could be as creative or as boring as you want. Thanks to Godfrey's inspiration, I have decided to give it a serious stab.

Similar to 80% of all Americans, public speaking is also one of my *favorite* hobbies. Let's hope that with enough sleep this can be done without too much stuttering.

Chapter 13: What's Wrong, Alan?

"Hey Ambrose, it's 7:15am already. We're starting devotion in a few minutes." A deep, strong voice emerged.

What the?!

Bob's voice was easily recognizable. How could he just barge in and wake someone up like that?

I took my time, sat up, rub my eyes, looked at him, and whispered with a poker face: "What time is it?"

"It's almost 7:30am. Everyone is waiting in the dining room." Bob responded softly but firmly. He didn't walk out after making that statement. He stayed in the room to make sure that I get out of bed ASAP.

Terribly intrusive. Baffled by his rudeness, I quietly gathered all the toiletries and clothes and, headed to the bathroom under Bob's escort.

Bob didn't exaggerate about how *almost* everyone was already waiting in the dining room. I was puzzled why everyone was so punctual and prepared, especially on an early morning. This had never happened before!

Oh yeah, it was the last day of work.

Anyway, time to get down to some serious business.

"Good morning everyone," I took the only empty seat left in the big circle placed against the door, "thank you for waiting. I assume we will begin our morning devotion first with an opening prayer, and have breakfast later like before?"

Arlene nodded.

"Hum hum," After a quick prayer, I cleared my dry throat the corny way to rid my nervousness, "let's turn to the book of Jude, chapter one, verse 17 to 25. That's the chapter right before the book of Revelation. It's a really short book in the Bible."

"The reason why I picked this rather unpopular book for this morning had to do with the fact that when Pastor Mick asked me to lead devotion a few days ago, I immediately said yes, but forgot that I have never done one before," Putting a disclaimer upfront while everyone else were flipping through the pages of their bible was better than doing nothing, I thought. "So I just randomly picked a scripture. Please excuse me if for whatever reason I did not make myself clear for the next 10 to 15 minutes or so."

Arlene smiled and nodded.

I smiled back and finished up on the introduction: "It turned out that the content in the book of Jude does have something important and relevant to this trip, as well as a lesson I've learnt from one of the many experiences I had here in Uganda. Without further ado, let's read the scriptures together:"

A Call to Persevere

"But, dear friends, remember what the apostles of our Lord Jesus Christ foretold. They said to you, 'In the last times there will be scoffers who will follow their own ungodly desires.' These are the men who divide you, who follow mere natural instincts and do not have the Spirit. But you, dear friends, build yourselves up in your most holy faith and pray in the Holy Spirit. Keep yourselves in the love of God, looking for the mercy of our Lord Jesus Christ unto eternal life. And of some have compassion making a difference; and others save with fear, pulling them out of the fire; hating even the garment spotted by the flesh."

Doxology

"Now unto him that is able to keep you from falling, and to present you faultless before the presence of his glory with exceeding joy, to the only wise God our Savior, glory and majesty, dominion and power, both now and ever, Amen."

I paused for a couple of seconds to make sure everyone finished reading the whole passage.

"Now, I understand that today is the last day that we will spend here. It has been almost 2 weeks already, and some of us may be getting a little homesick, while some may feel that there are still lots of things that need to be done. Either case, I believe that even though the short-term mission trip is coming to an end very soon, it's not the end of our responsibilities to evangelize and serve the needy."

"For myself, the last 2 weeks had gone by very quickly. Although I am personally mixed with different kinds of emotions and encountered various ups and downs, one thing I am pretty sure about is my conviction that whatever we have done or will do in the name of our God, they will somehow help. I can't specifically explain nor pinpoint how, but an event that I observed way back on the first day gave me the confirmation, and had encouraged me to uphold my purpose in life and remain focused."

Confession: I was naïve and felt that being didactic and speaking in grandiose terms would impress others.

"I don't know if you remember: after we got off the plane and got into the van that drove us all the way to here, the driver, let's call him "Mr. Chauffer", looked like he was in a hurry and was driving the van like a race car."

Nobody showed any signs of remembering that.

"Anyway, I was sitting at shotgun and felt the unexplained aggression. Not only was he speeding and cutting through traffic, at one instance he threw an empty water bottle out and murmured something that sounded like a curse. Of course, the cussing part was only a guess; whatever he said just didn't sound too friendly."

Still, the echo of my voice was louder than any other reactions. I decided to finish the devotion with one long shot.

"I was quite sure that his emotion had nothing to do with me or the team. But how should I respond? I wouldn't be surprised had we gotten into a crash, so I was concerned. Should I talk to him, assuming we could communicate and he will listen? Or give him a pad on the shoulder? Or do nothing and pray that we'll arrive at the destination safe and sound?

None of these options seemed appropriate. And as I was trying to find out the reason of his 'anger', I guess I could call that, I noticed that while we were waiting at JMS, the Joint Medical Store, and looking through the supplies, Mr. Chauffer sat at a table far away from everyone else, his right arm holding his lowered forehead, and he looked tired and depressed. And thank God, that was a perfect opportunity to step in.

It wasn't like I wanted to open a can of worms, so I did something very simple. It was getting hot, so I bought the team each a bottle of water, plus one extra one. When I handed him a bottle, which cost like a quarter, and about to say 'it's for you', he turned into an entirely different person: a fragile, harmless big boy and replied softly 'thank you'. Even though nothing had really taken place to resolve his issues, it probably helped to relieve his stress temporarily, from someone he didn't quite expect.

And the result? More than what I could imagine. I didn't ask for his help, but when we later got back to the van and continued our way to here, whenever I took out my camcorder to take a picture, he would lend me a hand by slowing down, making sure that I could take a good, clear shot. What's more, when we made a final stop at Mbale before we came here, I was trying to greet some of the children that gathered around us, but couldn't get through to any of them because of the language barrier. And guess what? Mr. Chauffer stepped in and played as translator. Note that we never really had a conversation, but I believe that it was God who did the work behind. Although there are definitely times when our efforts go futile, I do want to emphasize that going forward, be it during a short-term mission trip or in our offices at 3pm, we can all put some courage out and in faith to hope that God would bring out the best in all situations."

Second confession: This was merely something that sounded eloquent and supportive. At that time, I doubted if I could even believe in half of this rosy picture.

"With that, I would like to end the devotion by stressing that regardless of where we are, what we are doing, or how difficult the situation is, there is nothing to be afraid of if we are doing what's right."

Phew! This was much smoother than the time when I reiterated Tolstoy's story to Arlene a week ago.

Arlene waited for less than a second after the sound of my voice dissipated and asked: "Doug, would you like to close us up with a prayer?"

The clock at the background read 7:50am. It wasn't too bad, I thought.

Doctor Doug seemed a little surprised by what appeared to be an impromptu command, but still asked everyone to bow their heads.

After an unusually long pause, Doctor Doug began: "Father God, good morning." After another unusually long pause, he continued: "Thank you for this beautiful, sunny morning. We thank you for blessing each and every one of us here, who were brought together by you, to worship and praise you. We pray that you will bless the food and nourishment we are going to take, and give us the power and strength to continue doing your work today. In Jesus name we pray, amen."

Doctor Doug spoke in a very slow pace, and the prayer could not be more generic.

Before everyone jumped to the food, Arlene asked us to come back to this room at noon for a brief meeting to discuss, for the last time, about tackling Dorcas' and the clinic's needs, and how to allocate the resources we will be leaving behind. In the morning we could choose to do whatever we wished: play with the kids at Dorcas, pack up, rest, walk around, or just whatever. More importantly, she asked us to help look for a girl named Ida that didn't get to be examined by Doctor Doug for a complete physical check up a few days ago.

Arlene did not have a picture of her, nor could she precisely describe how she look either. She wanted us to "somehow" find a way to find her. Maybe we can ask around in sign language or Kiswahili? Malambe!

What should I do for the next 4 hours?

After gulping the final drop of the passion fruit juice, I decided to do a little bit of *everything*. That's what the term "last day" implies, if you ask.

First thing first: I felt compelled to check out the clinic one more time, to fight for the slightest chance to see Joseph one more time to let my heart rest easier. Then, of course, to just hang out and play with the children at Dorcas, whatever that would take, sure enough. After that, there were some bookkeeping items that needed to be updated. Finally, do some packing up, and make the final decision on what I could physically leave behind, other than the pair of black leather shoes that got all muddy during the last couple of weeks. The sole inside was wearing out, but they were definitely usable, if whoever finds them could just wash and clean them a bit and insert some soft padding. It's better than walking without any protection from the microorganisms hiding in the mud.

"Hey, I am going to stop by the clinic to look for Ida. See you all later!" I dashed without knowing who actually heard the lie.

♫"*One step more, one step more, give me faith for one step more…*"♫ the soft chant was endlessly circulating in my brain, forcing myself to feel more relaxed.

The hypnotism failed to work.

There was no medical staff at the clinic. Not even Jacqueline. As a matter of fact, there were no patients waiting outside of the ward either. Everywhere was as quiet as usual, without anyone in sight.

That was strange. More importantly, where was Joseph?

He must be inside the ward, resting peacefully and gradually recuperating. I was counting on Godfrey, even though trustworthiness became scarce ever since Conrad's appearance.

After a short and silent prayer, I headed over to Dorcas to try my luck on bumping into any kids I have met: mini Beyonce, Alan, or just any familiar faces that I could wave my hands to again.

I ended up waving my hands to Mark and Jon.

A little unexpected, it was still comforting to run into someone who I have not interacted for awhile. They were busy hosting a group game, so they just raised their eyebrows and nodded with a "What's up, dawg?" greeting.

About 15 to 20 elementary school age students held hands and formed in a big circle while hopping. The game looked terribly nostalgic from at least 15 years ago, but I couldn't recall the name of it. It was a girlish game mixed with charade, catch, and something else, and it was fun for most kids.

Soon enough, these quick actions generated an invaluable amount of laughter that burst into open air, and spread throughout the relatively quiet children center.

How I wished I had the kind of confidence, energy, and abilities to lead and direct like Mark and Jon.

Next time, next time; if I will ever have the chance to go onto another mission trip with more clues about the protocols and lessons learned from this experience, leading a trivial game at this magnitude shouldn't be a problem.

I grinned and almost laughed out frantically and sarcastically to myself. This was such a phony and meaningless determination.

Next to the big circle was a small group of boys that chose not to participate in this girlish game. No soccer game since the large group had already claimed the turf, but they appeared to be playing some undefined game spontaneously, invented by their quick wits, and thoroughly enjoying it.

No trace of mini Beyonce or Alan yet. I walked and turned in circles with my head kept stretching from left to right and up and down without any findings. Could the short interaction a few days ago indeed be a farewell?!

Relax, relax; this was supposed to happen like clockwork.

The perpetuating laughter circulating like a stereo system was a heartening reassurance. Everyone was doing fine as usual.

Everyone was as strong as ever. It was just plain simple joy that at times I fail to comprehend after started working in the corporate world.

The key concern at the moment for this establishment was the lack of tools and infrastructure that could sustain and prolong the community's subsistence.

Speaking of which, the final team meeting was scheduled later to discuss exactly that. My watch reminded me that I should slowly head back for lunch. I turned around at the gate, made a brief observation of the chaotic yet encouraging scene, shut my eyes tightly, took a deep breath of the cozy and muddy odor, and let the image and atmosphere transformed into microscopic pieces and sunk into my senses and memory.

The team will be back in the evening one more time for *the* final closing ceremony, so it wasn't quite over yet.

Mini Beyonce, Alan, and the rest of the familiar faces: I will be back very soon!

****

Pastor Mick was almost done collecting his clothes from the hanging liner right outside of our bedroom the minute I stepped into the courtyard. An old Japanese white truck with a dozen of small but colorful mattresses was parked in the courtyard.

"Hi Pastor Mick, any idea what these are for?"

"Oh hi Ambrose, I believe these mattresses were bought and delivered from Mbale for the boy's dorm. You know what kind of things they have been sleeping on." PM said softly.

"Yeah I know. Did someone go back to Mbale this morning?" I asked innocently.

219

"I think Arlene and Liz ordered them yesterday from the marketplace, among the other things they have bought. It was just that they didn't tell many of us." PM answered quietly.

"Oh I see." I proposed with a hint of skepticism: "So I guessed they have plenty of money to spend, after all?"

"That I don't know." PM coughed modestly, grabbed all his wrinkled clothes, and returned to our room.

Most of the ladies on the team were waiting patiently for the meeting to start in the dining room. A few were making small talks with each other. I grabbed an empty seat and remained silent. Soon, the leader and the other men came in.

"There is a change of plan for this evening. Because the children at Dorcas didn't have enough time to rehearse, Liz had decided to cancel the closing ceremony." Arlene made the announcement as calmly as possible.

The other team members somehow appeared as calm as Arlene. I was literally shaken. We have all learnt that random changes had been the central theme for this trip. Still, does it mean that there won't be another chance to hang out at the children center anymore?

"Instead, there will be free playing time for all the kids there, and you are welcome to join them if you wish. Dinner will be served early. We'll have to leave at around 5am tomorrow for a day-long drive. Will had already book the rooms at a hotel in Kampala, right by the airport. We'll be able to catch the early flight out of Entebbe to London the following morning."

Phew! You scared the crap out of me, Arlene!

Agnes brought in a few containers of food and Arlene had called a break. It was Will's favorite: fried chicken over rice with the thick, creamy Campbell soup gravy. Too bad he couldn't make it back for lunch though.

It was a speedy, down-to-earth, memorable, warm, and filling meal.

The meeting picked up seamlessly after everyone finished their bite. According to Arlene and John the treasurer, because no money was spent on lodging and expenses had been minimal, a large surplus was left on the budget (from the three grand we each paid) that could be used for a number of improvements. One urgent construction job that needed to be performed right away was to pave a large piece of asphalt on the seating area in front of the "stage" where the worship / drama / skits were held.

Everybody nodded at that proposal.

Next, Arlene casually mentioned the delivered mattresses, and some other rain gears they bought for Dorcas' staff with the team's excess savings. For the teaching supplies like drawing paper, crayons, and stationery, there were still some left, so Liz could take over and distribute them at the right time to the right people.

Nobody would dispute against any of that, even though the decision was made single-handedly behind closed doors and the "meeting" was merely an FYI.

After the short meeting was adjourned, most have decided to just hang out at Dorcas until dinner, including Doctor Doug, who worked at the clinic more than 90% of the time. When someone asked about my schedule, I told them that I haven't packed yet, and still had some bookkeeping stuff to do. I will join them whenever I am done.

"By the way, thanks for the devotion this morning. A lot of the stuff happening here is kind of like what you said." Brenda commented.

"Oh… you are welcome. I hope it helped." Surprised but not knowing which context she was referring to, I pretended to be cool, shrugged, and smiled on the inside.

Back to the dark and messy bedroom. Pastor Mick's stuff remained to be spread out all over his bed and Bob's old prison cell, kind of like me. Except mine were stacked on the front, along the side, and at the end of my own bed. If there were enough room in the bags to cram all of our belongings, the packing could take only a few minutes.

Well, space was a little tight. I will begin with the accounting job first. It was a breeze.

After sorting thoroughly and determining the most effective way to pack, two long-lost Murakami Haruki books resurfaced and caught my immediate attention.

Man, I need some closure. To prevent any more crap from happening again within the next 48 hours, the best way was to retreat to my bookworm comfort zone. I was 200% drained and could also knock myself into a nice long nap easily.

When I was about to lie down and enjoy a few short stories, the mosquito family, all 3 of them, were waving from the corner a few inches above my head. I jumped back up and resumed the packing process.

Let's see now…hmmm… 1, 2, 3, 4, 5, 6, 7, 8, and 9 pairs of undies. They are all here. They had been indispensable for some private comfort, albeit wrinkly and several pairs have transformed into a different color.

And here are some tees, shorts, and socks. All lacked softness after they were hand washed and naturally dried by Liz's maids.

What the freak am I doing? Screw this crap!

I jammed and squeezed all the apparels and other frivolous possessions in the luggage, closed the zipper, and dashed out to the ultimate destination. Without the bulky camcorder, it felt a lot lighter than before.

****

Damn, I missed out on more than 2 hours of fun.

No matter how you called it: a carnival, gala, or a farewell party, the crowd seemed to be- no, they *were* all having a blast from mingling with each other, playing games, or simply watching others socializing.

♪Music! Harmonica music ♪! Where did that come from?

It came from several feet away, right by the edge of the stage. Doctor Doug was the one playing the accordion! He had been bragging about his baby and complaining about how he had not had the chance to play yet. A bunch of small loyal audience were either squandering in front of him motionlessly or timidly dancing to the jubilant tone.

On the other end of the premise where the soccer field was, apparently, a soccer tournament was going on! It wasn't just any casual game. A small piece of blackboard titled "World Cup Qualifier Finals" with two teams named "Manchester United" and "Arsenal" written underneath. The score was still 0 − 0. It was Mark and Jon that were hosting the games. I doubted if they even took a lunch break.

The ongoing game was especially competitive and vigorous. Supporters of the two fictitious teams were cheering and clapping in the soccer-game-only rhythm and chant. The players were no

223

longer kicking the ball arbitrarily whenever they touch it, but ball hogging was obvious.

Suddenly, someone's hand grabbed my shirt at the waist level.

It's Alan!

It's not a mistake. He was still wearing the same t-shirt since the first time I met him!

Thank God for a perfect ending! I seriously thought it was just wishful thinking to ever see him again!

"Alan! How are you? How have you been this past few days? Do you miss me these days?!" I asked these meaningless questions and inadvertently gave him no time to respond.

Alan looked at me with his trademark smile, somewhat shyer than before.

"What do you want to do? Play some games? Or watch the soccer game? Did you bring any friends with you?" I continued my wave of questions and monologue in the same manner.

"*Cough cough!*" Alan's answer was quite unexpected.

Alan's cough sounded heavy. It sounded like he was holding a mouthful of saliva. It had to be mucus. It sounded like a pretty bad flu already.

I held onto Alan's little hand and walked together over to Doctor Doug. Alan's eyes were blinking innocently, waiting for whatever was going to happen next.

"Excuse me Doctor Doug," I interrupted in the middle of his play without any guilt, "Can you give me a hand and check to see if something's wrong with this boy here? He was coughing, and it sounded like it wasn't a normal cough."

Doctor Doug kindly took a break from his enjoyment and waved Alan to step closer. He then pressed on his face and looked at his eyes and tongue. Next, he put his hand onto his upper back. Meanwhile, Alan coughed again.

In less than a minute, the doctor gave his diagnosis: "He has a fever, and his temperature is quite high. Take him to the clinic and ask for a doctor for some treatment and medicine."

"Does he have any other illness?"

"Let the doctor there do a more comprehensive check up." Doctor Doug assured me of the best approach.

"Okay. Thanks Doctor. Let's go Alan." I reclaimed his little hand and smiled at Doctor Doug.

"You're a good man." Doctor Doug smiled back and returned to his accordion.

The compliment was unique and uplifting, but I was more concerned about Alan's condition.

****

It was a creepy scene if you visualize it: a young exotic Asian guy, probably the one and only one within the radius of 300 miles, along with a local boy about 5 or 6 years old, whom they have recently met but never had a conversation, were walking together away from a fun-filled, noisy carnival towards a far less pleasant place for a more in-depth check-up. The boy with the cough was *almost* as happy and jumpy as before, while the part-time guardian became more anxious about the unknown lying ahead.

The mud remained dry throughout the day. It still hasn't rained yet, but the 5-minute walk to the clinic felt like an eternity.

Alan's cough subsided a bit and he turned to me with a bright smile. He had no clue what was happening and was probably expecting me to bring him to a better place for more fun.

I smiled back but did not initiate the nonsense-talking. I needed to give myself some quite time to prepare for what the doctor may tell me soon.

What's the worst that could happen? Alan might have contracted some strange disease that would cause him to ache all over his fragile body. Or, he had a fever and needed to take some pills for a week. Alan looked like he was faring much better than Sam or Joseph.

It was hard to be optimistic in Africa.

Sip, sip!

Wung, wung, wung!

The fragrance of crap, the herd of buzzing mosquitoes flying all over Alan and myself, and the cunning brownish green lizard camouflaged on the sandy grass that gave us unwanted companionship made it even more difficult to move forward. Alan still appeared comfortable and waved at his neighbors, with a proud and dazzling smile.

The destination was slightly busier than the morning. A couple of adult patients sat in the reception room outside of the ward and waited quietly.

I searched around for a staff on duty and soon bumped into Roger, or Michael Jordan of Sironko, who was slowly coming out of the lab testing room.

"Hi Roger, here's Alan, he was coughing and I brought him to Doctor Doug at Dorcas, and he said that he has a fever and he advised me to bring him over to the clinic here to get some treatment. Can you or someone else help him now?" I hastily blurred out the who, what, when, where, and why to get Roger's full attention, hoping that he would treat Alan seriously and cure him immediately.

Roger starred at me, looking kind of thoughtful and amused. Unhurriedly, he asked me to take a seat and let him take over.

"Dneirfymgnioduoyerawoh?"

"Yakomai." Alan now looked a little uncomfortable, and still didn't seem to understand what was going on.

"Esleerehwemosniapniuoyeragnihguocruoytuobaeromtibe lttilaemllet??"

"Hcumgnihton."

The brief exchange led to a more thorough investigative process: Roger took a sample of Alan's saliva and examined it with a microscope, and performed other testing. I literally stood right next to Roger for the latest update. During the interim, I smiled at Alan and asked him, via hand signals, to wait in the exam room next door.

Approximately 10 minutes later, the final verdict came out.

"Ambrose, Alan has a fever. But more importantly, he also has malaria. I will have to give him a shot to cure the malaria first, then he would need to come back later for the fever. He will be alright."

227

Phew! A more urgent and life-threatening problem was detected, and Roger has the right stuff to heal Alan. Hallelujah!

"Okay, thanks for the good news. So what's next? Should we wait after you finish with the 2 patients outside?"

"I will tell the boy about this and give him the shot now so you can walk him back. You want to wait outside until we are finished."

"Sure, sure. <u>Thank you very much</u>!" I couldn't express my gratitude enough for this unwarranted privilege.

I returned to the reception room and acted as if I were waiting to see the doctor like the other 2 that were here before me. I took a peek and wondered if they have discovered the awful fact that Alan and I have cut directly in front of them for a non-emergency case. Their heads continued to bow without any facial expressions. Perhaps they did realize the situation but chose not to respond since there wasn't much they could do about it anyway?

At any rate, I felt ashamed and sorry for the intrusion.

"*Ahhhhhh!*"

My fruitless mental search came to an abrupt end when Alan's sharp scream of pain from the needle rang through the whole clinic.

"Thank God! He is saved now!" I murmured in relief.

Alan strolled out softly from the exam room with a large drop of tears hanging at the corner of his right eye. Boy, that pinch must have hurt.

I smiled and extended my hands to rub the back of his head. A perfect, soothing, and economical gift to hand out at the moment would be a piece of candy.

It was too late.

Alan kept walking straight and ignored my presence.

I gave up searching for that small piece of reward for his bravery and chased after him. Few of his friends showed up from nowhere.

"Oguoydiderehw??"

"Tatohstogi!"

"Yalpogstel."

"Yugyzarcsihttuobategrof"

Alan rejoined his buddies and jogged along.

"Al-" I yelled, and it was futile. He must have thought that I was some sadistic monster that took joy in seeing little kids cry. The scariest part was that he did not even fling his arm at me when I rubbed his head.

I stood at where I was, watched the back of Alan quickly disappeared. In a way, I thought it was a nice goodbye

****

Oh crap.

The lights went out in the dining room without any warning. And so was the rest of the guesthouse. Or maybe the whole town of Sironko and the vicinity became dark suddenly.

229

Power was usually cut off right around 11pm or midnight, and resumed at 5 or 6am the following morning. But like in many places where the supply of electricity was constantly inadequate, rolling black outs were implemented from time to time, and warnings are usually publicly announced in advance.

Perhaps an announcement wasn't made this time around.

The team was caught totally unprepared and sat in the dark in awe while chatting in the dining room. Will quickly brought in a large, rectangular back up lamp with 2 light bulb tubes that emitted a strong white radiance. The conversations remained fairly undisturbed.

The only problem was, after awhile, a herd of mosquitoes began to gather around the lamp and created some piercing buzzing noises. Everyone had to stay away and cuddled in a smaller half circle.

"Which team won the championship of the soccer tournament?" I joked.

"Don't know. They were still playing when we left." One of the ladies commented.

After watching Alan faded from my view in front of the clinic, I went strict back to the bedroom and finished up on the packing. The process turned out to be a lot less hectic, and there were still room left in the bag after carefully sorting and putting everything in.

The blackout positively created a romantic mood for the happy hour part of the evening. There were no candles, but the dimness produced the kind of tranquil and mystery that nothing else could really substitute.

We were chilling after a long day of outdoor activities and waiting for a feast to cook up for the "last supper". Thanks to the blackout, it looked like the extended happy hour could be quite lengthy. The time for departure remained at 5am the next morning as planned.

Esther, a cute, cheerful little girl whom Liz invited to join us, stole the spotlight of the night.

She was reportedly the daughter of a friend of our host that needed a ride to Kampala. It could not have been a better timing.

And this little pumpkin didn't show any shyness when interacting with strangers from aboard. The language barrier wasn't a problem either. She clapped and smiled whenever one of us played or hugged her.

Liz brought in another surprise a few moments later: several baskets of goodies with arts and crafts items like bracelets, necklaces, dolls, bookmarks, drawings on a piece of papyrus / plywood, paper weights, and some *really* artistic mini wooden sculptures.

They weren't gifts to us. We could buy them as gifts for someone back home.

These little things were reportedly hand made by a local woman's group. It was one of the few major ways for the stay-at-home moms to make a few extra bucks.

The ladies were especially curious. They were the first to claim a spot in front of the table to examine the treasures and discuss among themselves.

It was all good. Liz caught our psychology and we were happy to have fallen for them. The stuff in the baskets was sold 10 times less than $5.99 each, or the price of the exact same items found at some major retail chains in the States.

Meanwhile, it was my turn to play with Esther.

Dance? Sing? Play? None of these sounded fun anymore. Looking at the lamp from behind, a wicked idea popped up.

"Raw, raw, raw!!"

I stood up with my arms extended and hands folded like claws and opened my month as if I were a beast ready to devour any living creatures standing in front. Esther looked in my small, half-closed eyes, paused, screamed, and ran to the other side of the room.

Fortunately, she didn't scream on top of her lungs. No one else noticed the silly scene, and Esther grabbed the leg of a lady by the table for some false sense of protection.

I smiled and walked towards her with the same gesture. This time, Esther just looked at me, screamed, and stood there.

The lady busy picking her favorite ornaments turned around and figured out what was happening, so she put her concentration back to shopping.

Poor Esther, so I thought. As soon as I returned to my seat Esther came up to me, waiting for something to happen.

There I went again- this time, I took a better look on her cute face: there was absolutely no sign of fear when she screamed! Even though I wasn't pervert enough to believe that she enjoyed the game, she was undoubted amused.

I knew I wasn't equally as amused. The monster act was a projection of my latest encounter with Alan.

"Don't you think Cost Plus would have almost the same thing?" June asked her buddy.

"Probably." She responded.

My turn to shop finally came after the ladies decided that "probably" meant "absolutely". A perfect time to put a stop on the repetitively hideous and juvenile act.

There was no Cost Plus near where I lived. The ladies' realization put less stress on my decision making process.

There wasn't a whole lot of merchandises left. The ones that weren't selected were indeed quite extraordinary.

A hybrid of paperweight and sculpture bearing the size of a football helmet was crafted into a picture of some mountain, trees, and animals. Even if I were interested enough to have that displayed at the corner of my bedroom to collect dust, there wouldn't be enough room in the luggage.

Ha! Here's something totally ingenious: a black voodoo doll with a pair of big white eyes wearing a skirts with green and red stripes! It was small enough to fit in the palm of my hand, and it had this frightening facial expression that as if anyone touched it, s/he will be cursed for the rest of his or her life! One of my co-workers, an unmarried lady in her early 40's who sat at the cubicle behind me, put a similar doll on her desk so that whenever she got pissed, she would put the name of her worst enemy (which changes all the time) on a post it, stick it to the back of the doll, and poke, twist, squeeze, crush, needle, sit, spit, bite, step, and pound (not necessarily in that sequence) on it until she was satisfied.

Maybe I should also get one for myself too and hang it at my cubicle!

The less fantastic items sitting at the center of the table were something more practical. I picked up a few of the bracelets made of plastic beads and noted a piece of paper attached with a short paragraph introducing what the woman group was about. They were only about 50 cents each. I had a long list of those who made a contribution to my trip that I would need to follow-up after returning home. These little things would have been perfect!

After packing away the souvenirs and returning to the dining room, Esther became the center of attention again.

"Raw, raw, raw!" Kids never got tired of the same repetitive stuff. Esther came to me and I scared her off with the same mean and ridiculously nasty gesture 3 times in a row.

The adults did get tired of it though. Shirley and a few others frowned at me. I eventually stopped, not so much because of their frown. The drama was simply getting too dry and stale.

Watching her run around and bug the other adults that welcomed her with hugs and pads was sweet and inspirational. Personally, something was missing to complete the picture.

I couldn't help it. I needed to vent. If the closure doesn't happen soon enough, I'll become schizophrenic until I die.

"Hey Doctor Doug," I seized the right moment this time when he wasn't talking to anyone for a brief moment, "Thanks for your advice. I took that little boy to the clinic and the doctor said that he had malaria in addition to a fever, so he gave him a shot to get rid of the malaria first. Later, he would have to go back to for some medicine for the fever."

"Oh, that's good." Doctor Doug replied, "at least he is now immune to the common deadly disease."

"Yeah, but... I don't know, when I heard him scream and saw the tears that dripped down his face and he ran away from me, I felt like... I don't even know how I am supposed to feel."

"Those disposable needles are pretty rough, and they really hurt!" Raeanne eavesdropped and answered on behalf of Doctor Doug.

"Right, right," I gazed at Raeanne for a long second and lowered my head.

My eyeballs were running from left to right a million times per minute. Realized that I could no longer articulate the rest of my story, I whispered to myself: "***the most important thing was that he was saved.***"

My adrenaline was pumping quickly and quietly throughout my system, and it felt like I have finished running a mile in 4 minutes. I smiled speechlessly at both Raeanne and Doctor Doug, and returned to my seat and brainlessly watched Esther played with everyone else.

Power was partly restored in the neighborhood, but the guesthouse only received a small share of it. After playing with the switches a bit, Liz decided to let the kitchen keep cooking the food with a small flame, and all of us would be eating outside around a large rectangular table.

"All of us" referred to the team, majority of the medical staff that was not on duty, and a dozen children that helped with preparing the night's feast.

To maintain my sanity, I rolled up my sleeves and volunteered to move all the furniture.

The large open area between the kitchen and the dining room, the one where Will mistakenly believed that I was practicing kung fu on a warm afternoon, was packed with at least 30 people, many of which I have neither met nor simply couldn't recognize anymore. It looked like it would be a busy night of socializing.

Esther appeared to be somewhat relieved to see more folks of her age, and wisely ditched the hideous beast and ran towards her comfort zone.

A large rectangular table was set in the middle of the courtyard with chairs placed a few feet away it in a circle. Three long bleachers with a capacity of holding 4 adults on each were put behind a fleet of chairs on only one side. The adults were asked to take a seat on a chair, and I claimed a spot in front of the bleachers.

The arrangement promoted a festive mood, but didn't really facilitate any personal conversations without stretching our necks or yelled across the table. Many of the team members gave up and sat there silently to wait for dinner to start.

♪ *Hailed to the QUEENs!* ♪

Yes, it was "QUEENs" and no, nobody was playing or humming any music. Arlene finally came out from nowhere dressed in the same white traditional Ugandan gown that was presented to her as a gift of appreciation during the church service a couple of days ago. Liz was also wearing the same dress in a different size.

The men, including myself, weren't interested. And so weren't the ladies. That was odd, I thought.

By God's grace, the long awaited dishes finally took the stage with Agnes's diligent efforts. They were mostly carbs, and it was the ultimate feast that included all the food that showed up in various different meals: two large plates of fried rice, a plate of white rice, a stack of chapatti, large bowls of egg casserole, chopped spinach, avocado salads, matoke, tilapia, some chicken meat, and other dishes that I couldn't readily identify.

Darn, no lamb or goat!

Suddenly, the sky was gradually fulfilling its daily routine. Mother Nature had postponed the rain to the most undesirable time of the day.

The mist was refreshing, I must admit. No one else seemed to mind either. I looked up to the sky and pleaded: "*I haven't asked you much during this trip God, and You know that I am not hungry. In fact, I have rarely been hungry all my life, thanks to you. But these folks here had been working for hours for this meal, and I pray that none of their efforts would go to waste. Please. Please. Amen.*"

"Hey Ambrose, can I show you something?" Bob, after checking on his camera, turned to me and asked.

"Yeah, sure."

"Conrad came this afternoon while everyone went to the children center. I happened to be here again, and he dropped this envelope off for you."

"Wow. Amazing. He won't give up, would he?" I opened the envelope with a stern face and there was a short note saying that he needed more money for his "education".

In lieu of the cancelled closing ceremony, a small group of children gathered on the other side of the bleachers and sang a couple of song to celebrate our visit. They were also the ones that helped prepare tonight's banquet.

No more 30-minute skit in an unknown language. Thanks for cutting it to the chase!

The last supper eventually didn't start until around 8:45pm. Honestly, even though there were over 10 big plates of food on the table, the crowd outnumbered them by a ratio of 3.5 to 1. There wasn't enough food. Period. It was deceptive. I scooped a bite of everything and decided to redirect my energy to converse with the unmet local folks sitting close by.

Over a dozen children were sitting on the bleachers in front of me, silently and eagerly waiting for their turn. When it's finally their turn, only the most traditional foods were left: the gravy-like matoke and the damped white rice (thanks to the mist).

They didn't seem to have a problem with the quick disappearance of the meat and the veggie, and consumed the carbs blissfully. It was better than the free brownish beverages served at Dorcas every day.

After making some short small talks, I couldn't take it anymore. The kids deserved more than that, even though they didn't know better. The adults were cracking jokes and conversing as usual. I drank my food, called it a night, and headed back to the bedroom. The "last supper" didn't matter to me no more. It was almost 10pm anyway, and if I don't fall asleep before Pastor Mick did, I would be tossing and turning for hours.

Farewell Alan. Farewell Joseph, mini Beyonce, Sam, and everyone else whom I had greeted, made face to, and played with.

From Sympathy (pseudo) To Empathy

Chapter 14: Happy Hugging

Tuesday, May 6th, 2003 @ 5:00am

The last, last day here in Uganda.

Actually, not quite. The more accurate description should be "the last, last hour here in Sironko".

Falling asleep and waking up has been unbelievably easy for the past few days, thanks to the temporarily subsided stomachache, along with sticking to the doctor's recommended daily dosage to sleep 8 hours straight at night. And going to bed at around 10pm definitely helped. Although there wasn't much sleep quality to begin with, when people get used to something, they would gradually learn to adept to it and naturally be contended about it.

"Hey, where were you last night? We were playing a game and couldn't do it because you were missing." Bob asked, not as offensive as the previous morning.

"I went to sleep early coz I was tired." I kind of didn't lie.

"The doctors and the Dorcas staff gave us each an African name." Shirley interjected.

"Oh, really? So who's who?" She caught my attention.

"I had it written down somewhere… I will email everyone once we got back." Shirley appeared to be in a good mood.

"Oh please, I look forward to it." I wasn't lying at all.

Shirley kept her words and here's an abridged version of her email dated 5/9/03:

Sera - Arlene

Nambozo- Ambrose
Nandudu- Shirley (Humble)
Nambozo-Denise

Nam*bozo*... I wondered what that meant, and Denise shared the same name. And Nandudu meant humble. Very interesting! Shirley did mention that it was likely a mistake that "Nambozo" showed up twice, but that was what she had and she asked someone to send out a corrected list. No one did, so this must have been the correct version.

The sun already rose and it was bright enough to see without any lights. The same long rectangular table covered by the exact same blue cloth was stationed at the exact same spot with different breakfast items. It looked like they partied quite late last night and didn't even bother to put the table away. And thank God, it really didn't rain; nothing looked soaked or moist.

"What's that?" I took a close look at the tray Agnes was holding. It was some green fruits cut in quarters. They looked like huge dried limes. Were they really edible?

"Orange." Agnes smiled.

"Oh..." I took a picture of it and tried a piece. The fiber was poking my tongue, and I had to chew carefully.

"Okay everyone, let's take a group picture before we take off!" Arlene made a sensible suggestion.

The first group picture was taken at SFO before the team departed, I later found out. It wasn't a complete one since I didn't show up until 2 hours before the flight. To play safe, before the trip someone suggested to do a group check-in at noon at SFO, and everyone else showed up accordingly. The flight was at 6pm in the evening.

Agnes was invited for the picture too. We all loved Agnes, so the fact that we had never taken an official team picture didn't really bother anyone.

Jon and Mark woke up early to send us off also.

"Alright Jon, Mark, goodbye and don't cause any trouble!" Arlene joked as the team sat in the van after loading all the luggage.

"Yeah, yeah, yeah, just go!" Jon smiled back. He was always the humorous one, and nobody could tell when he was serious.

Two vans carrying the team, our hosts, a hired driver (Will was the other driver), and Esther (who could have forgotten her?) settled inside the vehicles and slowly drove off for the long journey.

I seized the last chance to take a good look of Dorcas when the van passed by. It was quiet and empty at 5:30am in the morning. Some birds were singing a soft hymn in the sky, which strengthened the exceptional aloofness of its serenity.

The long journey brought us to downtown Kampala in merely 7 hours, which was super fast since we didn't stop for a potty run or got out of the van for any stretching break. Will pulled into the parking lot of a school / church establishment and once we stepped out of the vehicles, the bright shining sun, the street noise, and the vibrant urban feel had literally brought us back to the long forgotten reality.

The first stop was to drop Esther off.

The little angel donned a light greenish dress and was as equally adorable as the prior evening, less jumpy and energetic.

"Raw, raw, raw!!!"

243

To make sure that she would remember me at least for a short while, I couldn't help but to remind her of the beast that she grew in love with and feared.

Her sharp memory did not deter her from running away from the big fat monster. As soon as she realized that she had ran too far away from the group, she would return and acted serious again.

"Oh, sugar pie, give me a hug!" One of the ladies requested and went ahead at the same time when it was time to say farewell, and others followed.

After everyone else was done, I squat down, smiled, and padded the back of her head. This time she flinched a little but didn't attempt to escape.

This should really be the last, last time I would talk to a kid during this expedition.

"Be a good girl and pray, okay?" There was really no point to babble a long sentence.

Esther nodded, a little appalled at the 180-degree change in the weirdo's behavior.

****

There wasn't much traffic in the part of town we were traveling. It took us only another 15 minutes to arrive at the next destination- lunch.

Will pulled into the parking lot of an outdoor café in front of a two-story building with a sign "Bible House" hanging in the front. The "café" was indeed a mini buffet restaurant, but the selection and portions were pitiful compared to the lavish meals we've been consuming at the guesthouse. Breakfast was very light and happened more than 8 hours ago, yet nobody seemed to have much of an appetite.

When our hosts noticed our inaction at a buffet, they made a wise decision to continue onto our journey.

There was another destination they really wanted to hit up before it was too late, and they had all the reasons in the world to do so: to go see their son.

The vans took a spin at the outskirt of the town to an even more desolated district, apparently a much better neighborhood and environment for studying.

Stood before us was a series of giant, straightly rectangular pale beige two-story Spanish villas with the slanted roof made with antique-looking red bricks. "London College of St. Lawrence (for a brighter future)" was inscribed on the large sign planted in front of the gated area. Once entered, 2 large touring bus with the same appellation (except for "for a brighter future") painted on the body were casually parked in the middle of the lot. When we exited our vans, the sun's reflection off of the finely polished white poles hanging the Uganda flag and the school flag literally blinded our eyes for half a second.

The parents hiked up to a fleet of stairs to the administrative building while the rest of us waited in the parking lot. Soon, a teenage boy wearing a white uniform with the school's mascot both on the tie and the shirt descended with his proud folks.

"Oh, this is your son, huh?" A lady went forward and started a conversation before our hosts made an official introduction.

I stood from the far side and observed the funny, clueless, reluctant, embarrassed, and "why-you-got-to-pull-me-out-in-the-middle-of-class-and-meet-with-a-bunch-of-strangers-whom-I-will-forget-their-names-and-faces-in-a-minute" face the boy had. Some students walked by near the lot, curiously gazed at the commotion and the small group of foreigners.

The mom finally let go of her boy after giving a dreading monologue, sweet hugs, and loving kisses. The rest of the team waved goodbye at the boy, who fled back to class immediately.

What a classic scene. What a sharp contrast to what we've seen for the past 2 weeks.

The relieved parents got more talkative and Liz tried to fill us in about our next destination: the bazaar. We got there before she could even begin the overview.

A picture is worth a thousand words: this bazaar was situated on a large piece of flat land with booths spread out around a smaller piece of grass land, and people could literally lie on their backs and sunbath as if they were in a park. The booths were miniatures of the Spanish villas we saw moments ago, except that the brick roofs were a lot flatter. Not a single foreigner was spotted, so the stuff the vendors were selling should be more authentic than those made by the woman's group.

And yes! I guessed it right this time without any surprises!!!

They had the generic souvenirs like postcards, tote bags, paintings, etc. as well as the daily essential items like clothing, toiletry, food, CDs, etc. It was like the marketplace in Mbale, but the quality of the merchandises and layout of the facility was noticeably more upscale.

Before we all jumped to scouting and enjoying the "fun" of bargaining with Will's and Liz's assistance, we needed to get some cold hard cash. We still had more than enough shillings that were exchanged at the bank on the very first day of arrival. I figured that if there were still any left after this shopping spree, I would just take the remainder and spend it at the airport on the last day, or donate it to our hosts.

To my surprise, most of the team members only wanted to exchange $5 or $10 worth of money to spend on gifts and souvenirs.

"Let's see now... who haven't I exchanged the money with?" I was tallying the total for the record and someone seemed to be missing. "Oh! Nurse Raeanne! Don't you need any pocket money?"

I looked up and searched all over the place; where was she?

After a few minutes of futile effort, I returned to the vans and asked for help. Will and a few others were hanging out instead of shopping.

"Has anyone seen Raeanne? I can't find her anywhere!" I exclaimed.

"Her friends picked her up and she said she is going to work in a clinic in DR Congo for a few weeks before going back to the United States." Will responded calmly.

"What?!" A few of us were astounded.

"How could she just left without saying goodbye?!" I was bumped; she was one of the teammates I could connect better with, especially after the small group sharing!

"I guess she just doesn't want to get into an emotion to say farewell." Allison commented after the dead silence went on for too long.

"Oh..." Remembering the kind of sentiments she shared when seeing a little boy die and there was nothing she could have done as a nurse, ditching the group like that might have indeed been a better choice.

After regaining my poise, I was convinced that there were more reasons to go shopping.

Half an hour later, nothing was really appealing: the arts and crafts were either too big to fit inside the luggage or too expensive (even by American standards!), and strangely they didn't have the conventional mementos like magnets, pins, or key chains either. I bought a few postcards, some mini drums, and wall ornaments for my folks and relatives.

And the music! How could I forget? Especially when I bought a pair of drums?!

The CD vendor next to our vans laid out a generous selection of music and compilations inside of a brief case on top of a folding table including gospel, R&B, rap, jazz, reggae, and even African classical. African classical?

I leaned forward and took a closer look...oh... they were all copied CDs; it was too obvious from the printing quality of the cover.

"Ten dollars! 10 dollars only, my friend! It's real African music!" The seller won't let me take the time to think it through. I did want some real African music, but not without a limit.

And Will came to the rescue!

"Rofesehtgnillesuoyerahcumwoh?"

"Orbhcaeskcubnetsti!"

"Ffoseimmohympirotyrttnodnamnoemoc!"

"Three for 10 dollars; pick whatever you want Ambrose, if you really want to buy them." The diplomat negotiated a much better deal.

That was fair market price. I recalled buying some elsewhere on another continent. It's always a gamble in terms of the quality though.

"I will take these 3." Not wanting to give the seller more time to lure me into other sketchy deals, I randomly picked a gospel, a reggae album, and a compilation of "authentic" traditional African music.

It was fun to enjoy the victory of bargaining when Will did all the work!

Soon, everyone finished shopping and returned to the vans, tired from running around under the sun and without much sleep.

"Alright, we will check in at the hotel now!" A much anticipated announcement was finally made.

We've arrived at a pretty decent inn right before 5pm after a quick 30-minute ride to Entebbe. The inn had a bar, a restaurant, and a staff holding a spraying canister to kill the mosquitoes. The price of a bottle of domestic beer was $2, which wasn't cheap at all by local standards.

Pastor Mick was again my roomie.

"Do you guys want to check out the neighborhood? We rented the van and the driver, and there's still time." Will had some good ideas at times.

He wasn't going to come along, which limited the potential "fun" we could have. Denise, Allison, Brenda, and I, the four that played around with the remains of the torn scraps and shared how we were "called" to this trip a week ago, went onto another round of adventure.

Will asked the driver to take us to some place safe. Too safe, in fact, that street block only had 2 shops opened for business: a grocery store and a woman's clothing store. One of the ladies found the apple of her eye there, so most of us waited in the van.

We kept quiet for a few long minutes, didn't feel like talking.

"It was quite a surprise, huh? When Raeanne just left like that..." I started talking.

"Yeah, but we have her email address, so it should be easy to keep in touch with her afterwards."

"What do you think about this trip?" I continued, trying to get some inside scoops that may coincide with my unspoken perceptions after pausing for a few seconds.

"It was good. I am just exhausted now." A rather politically correct and disappointing answer.

I stepped out and went to the grocery store to breathe some fresh air. They literally had everything a household needed, except for local coffee. I had been looking to bring home some freshly grinded Uganda coffee, but have only seen the packaged ones originated from Kenya.

Nothing worked out at the clothing store, and the driver took us back to the inn. There were still a couple of hours left until dinner, and the sun was still shining. This couldn't be all the sightseeing, could it?

"Hey Pastor Mick, are you going out for a walk?" Pastor Mick was pointlessly lingering at the lobby, appeared to be looking for something to do.

"Sure, I've got nothing to do. Should we all go somewhere?" Pastor Mick also invited Brenda.

The three of us walked out and noticed a flea market similar to the marketplace in Mbale across the street within walking distance. The chain of shops constructed by irregularly shaped pieces of wood covered by tin sheets and built on rugged rocks looked extraordinarily ghetto, but there's where the fun usually is.

Plus, if you were walking side by side with the big teddy bear, what's there to worry about?

The butcher was smoking and chopping on the torso of a fresh corpse next to the old lady selling apparel, and across from them a young lady turned up the pop music playing on a cassette deck, showing off the music selection she had in her booth. A few feet away was a shop barbequing some smoky meat. The smell of charcoal and food permeated the entire block, and everything is business as usual.

That was hardcore beauty.

What was more beautiful was that everybody left us alone. Freedom was pricey, but well worth pursuing it.

Fun times always passed by too quickly before you get to fully enjoy it. The sun was blinding our eyes as it sets. It was time to head back for dinner.

Our host booked a private room for all 13 of us. Liz sat on one end of the table with Arlene around the corner, and Bob next to Arlene. Shirley and June stuck together like twins as usual, and the rest of us, including Will, were sitting just wherever.

251

Liz waved at the waitress and asked us if we wanted fried rice or white rice.

"Oh, no, no, no, can you ask her to bring us each a menu?" Arlene was extraordinarily quick to stop Liz.

The mandate allowed us to order whatever we wanted: appetizer, soup, drink, entrée, or dessert. Couldn't complain about anything this time.

Oh! They have oxtail soup?! I wanna try!

I have also ordered a beef dish for entrée. But damn, the soup got some kick in it! The beef bullion was strong, and the chef probably put some indigenous spice into it. I couldn't tell what it was, but it's certainly addictive. Thank you Arlene, for the blatant request to Liz!

Normally, if I were famish, I would have picked up the bowl and poured the soup down my throat regardless of the temperature. I wanted to slowly enjoy the specialty, so one sip at a time with a spoon made do.

Yum yum! I finally figured out what that indigenous spice was!

It was a long lost friend of mine… Papa Mosquito!

The long, swinging leg assured me that it was indeed him! Entirely my fault for not saying goodbye earlier. He must have wanted to wave at me for one last time and hid himself inside the bowl to surprise me, and got cooked before it was too late!

Crap.

I lost my appetite. And so did the others, when they saw what I was playing with the spoon.

Among us all, Bob was the one that lost his appetite from the very beginning. He kept refusing to eat when Arlene kept asking him to order more. His slight anxious look suggested that he was not only exhausted.

He hasn't been the same since moving out of the bedroom more than a week ago. I wondered what might have happened.

Comfort of mediocre beds in a small inn magically dragged everyone back to their rooms instantaneously after dinner. We were advised that it could get dangerous if going out at night, and there wasn't much to see anyway. I tried to beat Pastor Mick to sleep as usual.

I lost. But thank God, PM was not making any noises or doing any magical tricks this time around, and my stomach was behaving properly even after drinking the yummy soup with extra protein.

****

No breakfast was served thanks to the early flight to London. The team was splendidly efficient when it came to air travel.

Thanks to Liz's sister, who worked at the airport and welcomed us there almost 2 weeks ago, showed up again to guide us the quick way to check in, going through security, etc.

While we waited for her and the hired driver at the inn, I walked out to catch a glimpse on what a typical weekday morning in urban Uganda felt like. Will came with me and pointed to the far side: "That's Lake Victoria, Africa's largest lake."

The attractive blue and the trees planted alongside the lake created a romantic compliment to the scene by the roadside. Pedestrians were either quietly walking on the sidewalk or waiting for a bus at the bus stop. The street wasn't crowded or noisy at all. There was a gas station on my left-hand side, and next to it was a short residential building. Some shrubs were planted in the middle of the road as a divider of opposite lanes. The infrastructure was well organized and preserved.

Liz's sister's effort in bringing us through check-in and security without hassle was however fruitless. When we got to the airport, everything literally stopped working. We were told to wait in the lobby after unloading the bags from the vans. Liz's sister went out of her way and discovered that the Ugandan king was also taking a flight out, so security heightened up and no other travelers could proceed before he finished.

To make matters worse, the airline's system went down when it was our turn to check in.

The clock was ticking real fast. We were still stuck at the check-in counter when it was time to board.

Ah, so what? This was so petty compared to all the stuff we've been through! I didn't mind staying another day and request for another PTO. My boss didn't schedule me to go out for another audit until the following Monday.

As my jokes continued to develop with my teammates about how we will be stuck in Uganda for several weeks without any more budget, the airline system came back to life, and a staff told the flight attendants at the gate to wait for us no matter how long it will take.

That was better; except that now we had to all swiftly run through the security checkpoint, which could take another half an hour for all 11 of us, assuming the guards were quick and easy going.

That was where Liz's sister came into play.

A new checkpoint was opened and served us exclusively. Each of us went through the metal detector and put our carry-ons through the screener as part of the standard procedures, but that was it.

"Go." A security guard with a poker face sitting on a chair gave us that order with a finger pointing towards the gate.

Our hosts had been waiting on the other side of the checkpoint to greet us the final farewell.

One by one, the team hastily shook hands with all 3 of them, and thanked for their hospitality and the experiences.

"Hey Will! Thanks for hosting us. I had a great time in Uganda and looked forward to come back if I can!" A little unprepared for the quick goodbye, I pushed to communicate the most positive and sincere message out of my system.

Will was speechless.

"And I'll…" Suddenly, Will interrupted with his arms wrapped around my back. I instinctively hugged back.

Tick, tick, tick, tick, tick, tick, tick, tick, tick, tick.

Ten seconds had elapsed, and Will showed no sign of letting go. It was an unusually long hug between 2 guys, unless…

"Okay, Will…" I edged back slightly, but Will shut down the signal and hugged even closer.

Tick, tick, tick, tick, tick, tick, tick, tick, tick, tick.

"Already, Will, we must leave now." I padded his shoulder lightly and he steadily let go.

"Take care now." I gushed out the final words softly, and Will remained silent.

****

The clashing coins in my pocket reminded me to do something very important as I kept running towards the boarding gate. I looked around and found a place where the money could be dispensed. John and someone else were still behind me, so it was worth a shot.

I stormed into the souvenir shop, found a magnet with Uganda's national anthem printed on the top, used up all of the shillings, and claimed my aisle seat on the plane in less than a minute. I was way too happy to have succeeded in taking that risk!

Except for a small miscalculation: John and his companion caught up and passed me within that minute, which made me the last person that boarded the plane while everyone was curiously watching.

Ah, what did it matter, I got what I wanted!

"Are you alright?" Bob saw me wheezing with joy.

"Yeah, I just made a stop at a gift shop and grab the last chance to buy some souvenirs!" I took the magnet out and dangled it for some interested onlookers.

"Oh, I wanted one too!" Bob looked covetous.

"Well, that was just to spend all the Ugandan shillings I had in my pocket" I regretted to be a little cocky.

The other onlooker was a neighbor sitting by the window, the one and only Ms. Brenda! It wasn't until then I realized that we had yet a one-on-one conversation about anything.

In fact, there hasn't been many, as I recalled, one-on-one dialogues in general between me and any team member. Conversations had been either shallow or in a group setting. Sometimes, even if there seem to be a chance to talk a little deeper about the trip itself or personal things, I didn't know how or where to begin.

"Ladies and gentlemen, the featured film of this flight is "Catch Me If You Can", starring Leonardo DiCaprio and Tom Hanks. Please sit back, relax, and enjoy the movie. Thank you."

The announcement interrupted my train of depressing thoughts and redirected me to the film I have always wanted to watch. It didn't matter if it were a non-fiction story or not. The cast, plot, and sequence of events were all ingeniously calculated and produced.

Unfortunately, my fatigue kicked in and the movie was over 135 minutes long.

"Ladies and gentlemen, may I have your attention please: this is the captain speaking. We are now flying above Chad and the Safari Desert is right underneath. If anyone is interested in taking a good look, you can lift the shades and enjoy." Another deafening announcement intruded and woke me up from a nice sweet nap, but it was a piece of exciting news.

"Brenda, can you lift the shade and let me see the Safari Desert?" I couldn't miss this chance to take a good picture.

"Sure." Brenda put her book down.

"Wow, isn't it awesome?" The blue sky was crystal clear and the desert looked more like a gigantic sandy beach.

"Hey, you see that two black spots in the middle of the desert? What do you think they are?"

"Don't know, it could be a caravan or just an eagle. We are like 10,000 feet above ground now." Brenda's suggestions couldn't be too far off the line.

"Or they could be undiscovered oases." Brenda and I both laughed at this impossibility.

The flight arrived smoothly at Heathrow in mid-afternoon on a weekday, and the lines to go through immigrations were relatively short. The officers at the counters were working professionally.

"Hi." I handed the uncompromising-looking guy my passport with a trademark chubby smile.

After 15 seconds of page flipping and intense inspection, in a deep voice he asked: "What were you doing in Uganda?"

"Vacation." That was partially true.

"It's not the tourist season right now!" This guy detected my lie and pushed forward to make the felon confess.

"*Because I feel like it, butthead!*" The devil on one shoulder provoked me to respond in the same manner. The angel on the other shoulder prompted me to tell him the truth that I was in Uganda helping out in an orphanage. My instinct to play dumb and act innocuous at critical moments activated, so I kept my mouth shut.

The genius finally figured out that he might be wrong about something, so he tossed my passport back.

"Thank you officer." I adopted his way and responded softly and sarcastically.

"What's taking so long?" Bob asked. The rest of the team had already passed through the check point.

"That immigration officer was questioning me like a criminal. He almost won't let me thru." I didn't exaggerate.

"That's mess up man, that's wrong." Bob was utterly surprised. I felt better after venting the crap right away. It didn't matter who I spoke to.

Finding the way to the Holiday Inn hotel nearby with our reservations presented another immediate challenge.

When the team passed by the airline's customer service counter, Brenda stopped and tried to speak with an attendant.

"What's going on?"

"I am trying to see if they can change my flights so that I can fly home directly from here instead of going to SFO and then back to the east coast." Brenda's point was legit.

"Was that how they booked your ticket?" I was baffled at the arrangement.

After explaining the situation to a staff for at least 5 minutes to no avail, Brenda and a few of us gave up and rejoined the large group, whom were still trying to find out which Holiday Hotel the reservation was made.

Shirley and June took the lead and walked towards the opposite direction of where the group was heading.

"Where are they going? Did they figure out the way?" I looked around while asking innocently.

"To the hotel."

"Are they staying at a different hotel?" The twins were walking away briskly and didn't care if anyone else followed.

"No. We're all staying at the same hotel." Doctor Doug forgot to smile.

"Then why-" I stopped the questioning almost too late.

This is unbelievable! The team couldn't wait to be dissolved, and I thought the twins and Arlene were homies all this time!

The difficulty to get to the hotel did not diminish after the twin's departure. Reportedly, there were two "Holiday Inn Hotel Heathrow" and the booking confirmation did not specify which one it was. Yet even if we eventually figured which is the right hotel, how do we get there? No one had any pounds to pay for a shuttle or a taxi!

Geez, shouldn't these logistics stuff be all planned and verified beforehand? We are not in Africa anymore! I couldn't help but to shake my head.

This time, Doctor Doug came to the rescue.

He managed to call a friend of his daughter and she gave him the lodging confirmation and direction. It was within walking distance and Frances, our Samaritan, even agreed to come to the hotel later and join us for dinner!

How did Doctor Doug manage to find a phone or some coins to make the call? That I didn't know.

The embarrassing moment came after hiking for a mile with our carry-on to a classy-looking hotel, and after some conversations the clerk at the check-in counter told us that we were at the wrong hotel! He however had agreed to transfer us to the right hotel via the hotel shuttle. We have finally reached another transit point safely and beat the twins to it!

So much for the never-ending adventure.

Frances subsequently came to the right hotel and hooked up with Doctor Doug. She had generously offered to drive some of us around town and to dinner. For some strange reason the doctor decided not to go out after meeting with Frances, but asked her to be the chauffer and tourist guide for some of us. The twins and Denise said they wanted to catch a London sightseeing tour bus if possible. John, Pastor Mick, and Arlene preferred to spend a quiet evening inside the hotel.

That left Allison, Brenda, Bob, and I to fit inside of Frances' little Renault. Perfect! And I wouldn't pass on the opportunity to stick with a local for a free private tour!

The 5 of us went to an Irish bar nearby for some drinks and snacks. The fun escalated when the menu indicated that the bar also served full course meals. The superior grill with double portions of sirloin steaks, sausages, ham, bacon, baked potatoes, eggs, and black pudding sounded tempting.

"What's a black pudding? Is it like a dessert or something?" I turned to the new host with an innocent look.

"It's different types of animal blood mix with some kind of meat." Frances proudly introduced the delicacy.

"Cool!"

When the plate came and the meats were stacked a mile high, I realized that there was way more meat than what I had consumed within the last two weeks.

261

"Alright Ambrose, you convinced me!" Bob snatched a piece of the pudding after seeing me swallowing the meat like a bear.

The night was still young by the time we got out of the pub half satisfied. We asked the volunteer to drive us around to shop for some souvenirs.

Poor Frances, stuck with a bunch of strangers, did her best to put up with us and took us to a large supermarket so that we can bring back some snacks for our co-workers and families. But of course, we were all adults and got along fine.

Sometimes, what goes around does come around. And when it doesn't, someone would be sent from above to balance the flow. Call me superstitious, but it had been an amazing experience to see how God had always been so graceful even when the immigration officer was otherwise.

For the very last night, I still had no idea how the rooms were divided. This time, Pastor Mick claimed his own room and Bob became my roomie.

A little mean to say, but Raeanne's early departure practically helped to divide the rooms more evenly. Else, a guy and a gal might end up having to share the same room for the night (the ratio was 7 gals to 5 guys). And I doubted if the budget would have allowed 2 extra rooms.

"Go ahead Bob, why don't you use the bathroom first. I will probably have to spend a long time in the shower afterwards." I didn't mention anything about not having showered for almost a week.

The itchiness on my torso expanded exponentially once I learned that the opportunity to take a normal shower would only be a few moments away.

"Ahhhhhh!!!!"

I spent almost an hour in the hot steam and used up all the soap, shampoo, and conditioner to cleanse and rub all the dirt out. It felt like a pound of me was washed off permanently!

Bob was watching the BBC news attentively. There was a report about how some engineer working in Silicon Valley had to sell his house and BMW and go back to square one because of the poor employment conditions in the hi-tech industry.

"You know what, it's true. It's pretty tight now and there aren't *any* openings in the whole bay area." The engineer in front of me elaborated.

Good thing was that banking, especially wholesale lending, was still doing alright. I hoped Bob was doing alright at his job too.

Another night passed by peacefully and the trip was wrapping up quickly. It was exactly how things should look like before a perfect storm.

****

1, 2, 3, 4, 5, 6, 7, 8, 9... two more people were missing???

The team gathered in the hotel lobby right before 8am and found out another surprise.

Wait- I forgot to count myself, but Pastor Mick was indeed missing. It was obvious but nobody seemed to really care or asked his whereabouts.

He said he needed some quiet time, and that was why he claimed a room of his own. Did that have anything to do with his disappearance???

263

"Pastor Mick said that he already went to the airport to make sure that we will check in without any problems." Arlene declared.

"*Huh?*" Wow, that was really not a good sign. I will ask him personally when I see him later.

While the team was checking out from the hotel, Arlene told John and I, the treasurer and assistant treasurer, respectively, that Doctor Doug was going to pay for the rooms with his credit card, so to make a note about the exchange rate on the books and records accordingly.

"See, the conversion rates are posted behind the counters." Arlene pointed and showed to help us get a grip.

I turned around and was puzzled: "But wait, that's different, and why would Doctor Doug need to use his credit card? Weren't the rooms already been paid for?" I felt that I was entitled to some clarifications.

Arlene, maintained her gracefulness although slightly in awe, said: "Ambrose, I am not going to argue with you." She then slowly walked away. John saw the conflict and walked away as well.

I couldn't believe what just happened, among all the other surprises within the last 5 minutes!

We found Pastor Mick standing at the airline counter speaking with an attendant. The whole section was crowded with 10,000 people waiting in lines.

"Hey what's up? You are early!" I tried to sound informal.

"Oh, hey, I wasn't feeling comfortable about our tickets, so I got here early to make sure everything was alright."

"Is everything alright?"

"No, good thing that I came early and found out that the tickets we were holding were actually receipts. The seats were booked, but we needed the valid docs, and this lady here had been helping us." Pastor Mick was overwhelmed, and so was I.

What the heck was the travel agency doing?

"So are we good now?" Let's focus on making some lemonade out of the lemons thrown at us.

"Almost- yeah." Pastor Mick grabbed a stack of paper from the lady but still didn't sound too relieved.

I seized and secured my boarding pass at once, and went off to a fast food chain alone for some lamb sandwich and a grape juice drink for breakfast to cool down.

A little bit of retail therapy helped too. All these times I thought it only worked for ladies. I bought a set of 20 mini die cast models boxed in a prepackaged display case, and felt more rewarding temporarily.

The time for boarding came right before I got tired of lingering at the giant shopping mall inside Heathrow. At the gate, Bob was playing with his camera and checking on the pictures he took.

"You see Ambrose, this is such a perfect picture to show the people back home." Bob showed me the picture of Joseph, the severely malnourished dying boy, while we were waiting in line to board.

I heaved a sigh to control the embedded emotion and enmity overflowing from the top of my lungs, then commented quietly: "Well, I really didn't think that it was a right moment to take a picture of him."

"THAT'S ONLY WHAT YOU THINK!" Bob yelled back without hesitation.

Every adult, child, man, woman, toddler, baby, living and non-living organisms at Heathrow heard the shout and tried to find out what was going on.

Confession: the response I gave could have been phrased less offensively, but I couldn't help it.

When I looked around to see who else wasn't affected by this shameful fiasco, I caught Arlene's reaction and she nodded.

She thought I was asking for her approval.

Alright, this is it; you people can all go screw yourself!

The best mistake that the travel agency made for all 4 flights of the trip, intentional or not, was booking the team to sit in different rows, and it was absolutely wonderful to be in solitude for the next 10 plus hours.

Bob probably felt bad for the garbage he yelled out earlier, and came to my seat and said that if he ever goes to San Francisco, he will go hang out with me.

"Oh sure, absolutely; no problem." This was the exact same answer I gave to my boss a few weeks ago in his office before flying out. The only difference was that my blood refused to boil.

A nap, a movie, and a couple of meals made the 10-hour wind down like a breeze. And the trip was going to come to a complete end at SFO very soon.

Mid-afternoon on a weekday at SFO was anything but busy. The ampleness of empty space allowed my dad and oh! My mom too! To spot me right away in the waiting area of the arrival hall after we cleared custom and immigration.

"Hi dad! Thanks for picking me up and mom! You skipped work today?" I needed a hug from them badly.

Sniff sniff… "Son, you need to take a shower." That was mom's first reaction to my much needed consolation.

I immediately let go of her and turned around to hug Bob, adding a few extra rubs on his back and applied the tight, suffocating hug in the San Francisco way.

June, the next person in line by chance, tried to avoid me but failed.

After some of my scent diluted, I approached some other teammates for some die hard sincere hugs and handshakes. The phoniness came to an end when I decided to keep a distance from those I became indifferent to.

Here comes Tori- oh yeah, Tori was Bob's fiancé, and she worked at FCA. It was one big family.

A flashback of Will's long hug naturally reappeared in my head, and its significance became evident.

That was a happy hugging indeed.

****

It was 5 minutes passed 6pm on a sunny but chilly Friday evening, typical San Francisco weather in late spring.

Most people have already left for the weekend, making the office even more desolated than any other time.

A bulky file was sitting on my desk. It contained all the relevant documents for my next assignment scheduled to start on the following Monday.

I stretched, yarned, and burped at the same time, but soon realized that it would have been easier to visit the bathroom for a final run instead, before leaving for weekly fellowship at 7:30pm.

The baggy pants conveniently slipped as I quickly unbuckled the belt and claimed the clean, unoccupied throne after slamming and locking the door.

Nothing but gas. Probably should have taken the time to chew the pre-dinner snack rather than to swallow the sandwich in only a few bites.

I pull down 6 pieces of the extra thick toilet paper to make sure that I am clean. The motion detector sensed my gestures and the toilet flushed robotically in one strong shot.

I put one hand underneath the faucet, the other underneath the touchless soap dispenser, and slowly washed my hands in the sink. I then turned to the side, held up my palms, and let the long paper towel rolled out. I looked into the mirror to fix my hairdo after tossing the paper towel. Suddenly, I couldn't recognize the stranger in the mirror.

A gush of blood surged onto the face of the reflection on the opposite side. He sighed, paused, closed his red eyes to prevent the water from flooding, and opened the door.

Luckily, nobody else was in the bathroom at that time.

A strange smile was hanging on his face as he stepped out of the office elevator and hurried to an evening of worship and fellowship.

-THE END-

Ambrose Tse

Epilogue

Did all these really happen?

That was the first questions that came to my mind. So much had happened and they happened so fast that they looked entirely surreal. It took me more than 4 years to understand and digest the kind of emotions and interactions involved. The only immediate celebration made was the sheer fact that I lost almost a pound a day during my stay in Uganda, only to gain it all back in 5 months.

For the first 10 months since coming back home, I was in complete limbo. Overwhelmed by the apathy of those around and the general wasteful nature of the American culture, at one point I thought about quitting everything in the U.S. and return to Uganda for good. Subsequently, thanks to the extended hands of those who took a chance to proactively exert encouragement and the support at a mission conference 9 months late, I came to recognize that I have encountered something called "reverse cultural shock". Simply put, it was a known issue that happens to those who ended up appreciating the other culture more than his or her own upon returning from a trip. The cure was simple: I spent a couple of days in solitude to debrief the experiences, piece by piece, and have made other commitments to refocus on the bigger picture to help the marginalized. Some of them included, but not limited to: increased monthly child sponsorships, joined other short-term mission trips on an annual basis if possible, document this transformational experience, and not to waste food (although it sounded petty and "helped" me to stay as a chubby guy). The path to these journeys, especially in the subsequent trips, posted different types of challenges and created even more surprises. Hopefully I will get a chance to share them in the future.

Up to this day, sadly, I have not kept in contact with any of the team members. Not even once. I later learned that intra-team conflicts were the undocumented leading cause of most discontinued mission projects, and it led me to realize that nothing is really new under the sun.

Last, I must reiterate that I have not become better equipped in making a difference in other people's lives. All I could say is that I feel blessed to be able to secure the luxury of helping others as a priority, which is something that most of us also have, but just haven't quite taken advantage of it yet.

From Sympathy (pseudo) To Empathy

Made in the USA
Columbia, SC
17 February 2025

54015533R00150